I0622175

The Asshole Who Didn't Want to Celebrate Christmas

ANDREW CASEY

JOANNE HENZLER

Copyright © 2024 Hypersanity Books

Paperback: 978-1-964744-65-0
Hardback: 978-1-964744-66-7
eBook: 978-1-964744-67-4
Library of Congress Control Number: 2024915403

All rights reserved. No part of this publication may be reproduced, distributed, or transmitted in any form or by any electronic or mechanical means, without the prior written permission of the publisher, except in the case of brief quotations embodied in critical reviews and certain other noncommercial uses permitted by copyright law.

This Book is a work of fiction. Names, characters, places, and incidents either are the product of the author's imagination or are used fictitiously. Any resemblance to actual persons, living or dead, events, or locales is entirely coincidental.

Ordering Information:

Prime Seven Media
518 Landmann St.
Tomah City, WI 54660

Printed in the United States of America

This book is <u>NOT</u> dedicated to whingers, two-faced bitches, toxic positivity promotors, twats, Christmas hater Assholes, Assholes and relatives enabling Assholes every Christmas.

ABOUT THE AUTHORS

Andrew Casey and Joanne Henzler work in geriatrics while interviewing forty people of all ages and various walks of life to write this story. To our surprise this story is not far from fact inspiring more Asshole and Crazy Bitch stories are in progress for years to come.

TABLE OF CONTENTS

RAVENSCROFT LANE

In the festive twinkling Christmas light filled neighbourhood of Ravenscroft Lane, jolly carols filled the air. One man had full intention to keep his traditions whilst sharing and embracing diverse traditions of others. But little did he know, his family's arrival on Ravenscroft Lane would ignite a holiday frenzy that even Krampus himself would not be able to control.

Meet Mark Garrison, The Self-proclaimed People Pleaser Who Wants to Celebrate Christmas." Mark has a wife who has a penchant for extravagant decorations and two teenage daughters are eager to start a Christmas shopping frenzy. Mark was soon to discover that resisting the yuletide spirit was easier said than done.

It seems biggest thorn in Mark's side was none other than his dashingly charming over-the-road neighbour, a grumpy old asshole who had zero intentions of embracing any kind of holiday cheer. As Mark's neighbourhood embarked on its annual Christmas festivities and traditions, tension rise, friendships are tested, and sides are taken. Will Mark succumb to the charm of Ravenscroft's Lane Christmas Traditions, or will Mark change the neighbourhoods' traditions to better suit his entitled millennial daughters? Join the uproarious holiday hijinks on Ravenscroft Lane, where spirits clash and the festive season is the greatest season of all.

CHAPTER 1

FRIENDLY NEIGHBOURHOOD ASSHOLE

Mark Garrison stood at the top of the driveway, his eyes scanning the quaint neighbourhood of Ravenscroft Lane. The lane was lined with charming, well-maintained houses, their brick exteriors and manicured lawns exuding an air of tranquility. A slight smile tugged at the corners of Mark's lips as he took in their new surroundings. This was going to be their fresh start—a chance to create a home that was finally perfect for his wife, Melissa, and their two teenage daughters, Candy, and Shirley.

With a deep breath, Mark turned and walked back towards the moving truck parked along the curb. He found his meddling Melissa, a vivacious woman with a warm smile and an infectious laugh, supervising the movers as they carefully unloaded their belongings. Her excitement was palpable, her eyes sparkling with anticipation of the new memories they would create in their new home.

"Mark, have you seen the girls?" Melissa asked, turning towards him with a worry in her voice.

"No, they're probably upstairs, busy making the place their own," Mark replied, casting a glance towards the grand two-story house that stood at the end of the street. "Remember your therapist told you to stop being a saggy-naggy helicopter wife micromanaging everyone. Why don't you go check on them? I'll help the movers."

Melissa nodded appreciatively before heading through the front door, her footsteps echoing in the now-empty house. As Mark unpacked boxes and directed the movers, his thoughts wandered to their decision to move to Ravenscroft Lane. It had been a difficult decision to uproot their lives from the bustling city they had grown accustomed to. But with the girls heading off to college in a year, they longed for a change—a place where they could reconnect as a family once more before the girls flew the nest. Unless Candy was to be held back another year since she was already going to graduate on the same day as her twentieth birthday.

Just as Mark was lost in his thoughts of his daughters' disappointment, a voice pierced the air, shattering the peace of the neighbourhood. "Hey, you! Do you even know how to park that van properly?" the voice boomed, carrying a tone dripping with sarcasm. Mark's eyes snapped up, his gaze landing on a staunchly built man standing across the street.

Dressed in a mismatched Hawaiian shirt and worn-out blue blizzard camouflaged pants, the man bore a striking resemblance to a tosser of a boss he had in a factory job years ago. He had a permanent scowl etched on his face, and it seemed like he was born to complain. Suppressing a sigh, Mark made his way towards the man who had become their first neighbourly encounter in the tranquil Ravenscroft Lane. The sight of him made Mark doubt his decision to move there.

"Uh, sorry if we parked the van in the wrong spot. It is the removalists not me," Mark apologized, his voice filled with genuine sincerity.

The man seemed to soften slightly, his scowl easing just a fraction. "Well, just make sure it doesn't happen again. Ravenscroft Lane has rules, and we expect everyone to follow them."

As Mark watched the man retreat towards the upper hill of Ravenscroft Lane, something piqued his curiosity. Across the road hidden behind a cluster of tall trees, was a large, dilapidated Victorian house. Its peeling paint and untamed garden gave it an eerie appearance, reminiscent of something out of a horror movie. Mark could not help but wonder who lived there.

"Name's Tom Henderson," he grumbled, irritation evident in his voice. "And if you plan on making it in this neighbourhood, you'll need to follow the Ravenscroft Lane Christmas Tradition."

"Christmas tradition?" Mark asked, curiosity lacing his words.

"Yes, tradition," Tom replied, rolling his eyes. "We're expected to prepare for Christmas in this neighbourhood, even though Halloween was just yesterday."

Mark could not help but smile at Tom's exasperation. The man had strong opinions and did not hesitate to voice them. But beneath his gruff exterior, Mark sensed a longing for something more—a sense of community.

"Is it a big celebration?" Mark asked, genuinely interested in this intriguing tradition.

Tom shrugged dismissively. "For some. But not for me. You see that old place over there?" Tom pointed towards the eerie Victorian house that had caught Mark's attention earlier. "That's Mr. Fredericks' place. Been living there for decades, and he has never celebrated a single occasion. Not even Christmas. We never agreed about Christmas."

Mark's eyebrows furrowed. It seemed unusual for someone to forgo any celebration, especially during the holiday season. But he reminded himself that everyone had their own reasons and traditions.

"Well, I guess different people have different ways of celebrating, our family have our own tradition inspired by an antique advent Calendar," Mark replied, trying to find common ground.

Tom snorted. "Yeah, not like old Mr. Fredericks cares about celebrating anything. But pay attention, if you ever decide to have a Christmas light show, just know it will not compare to mine. I am a twenty-three-time winner of the Gwenvale Christmas Light Contest," he bragged, a touch of pride creeping into his voice.

Mark chuckled, appreciating Tom's competitive spirit. "Well, I will have to make a mental note of that. But for now, I think we will focus on settling into the neighbourhood first."

"Almost forgot to give you this," Tom grumbled, thrusting the clipboard towards Mark.

As the moving truck drove away, Mark found himself alone on the porch, the brisk autumn air sending a shiver down his spine. Mark took the clipboard and glanced at the neatly printed papers. It was a safety checklist for the holiday season, complete with recommended Christmas ornaments and decorations for the impending snowfall. He could not help but marvel at Tom's meticulousness, though a part of him felt slightly overwhelmed by the level of detail.

"Thanks, Tom. Our decorations are up to par," Mark replied, extending a friendly smile.

Tom nodded curtly and walked away without another word, disappearing into his own house at the top end of Ravenscroft Lane. Mark could not shake the feeling that there was more to Tom than met the eye—an underlying desire for connection woven into his gruff demeanour.

Deciding it was time to explore beyond their own property, Mark walked across the street toward the old Victorian house. Taking a deep breath, he approached the door, the paint chipped and faded, as if it had been weathered by time itself. Raising his hand, Mark hesitated for a moment before knocking.

After what felt like an eternity, the door finally creaked open, revealing an elderly plumper man than Tom Henderson who looked like he had just stepped out of a classic detective movie. His frown was as deep as the lines etched on his face, and a mole he was cursed with just that was above the left side of his lip.

"What do you want?" the man asked angrily.

Caught off guard, Mark tried to collect himself. "Good evening, sir. My name is Mark Garrison, and my family and I just moved in across the street. I wanted to introduce myself and extend a friendly gesture."

Mr Fredricks slammed the door on Mark an uncertain mix of disappointment and determination swirling within him he quickly realized that Ravenscroft Lane had its fair share of challenges putting his resolve to make it a place of warmth and community to the test. "Well, that was rude," Mark said surprised. Now I know how Jehovah Witnesses feel every time I slammed the door in their face or got them with the soaker hose on a cold winter's morning.

As he walked back to his own house, Mark made a silent promise to himself—that he would not allow one setback or the enigmatic nature of Mr. Fredericks to dim his optimism. He understood that building connections and fostering a sense of togetherness would take time, patience, and understanding.

As the moon cast a soft glow over Ravenscroft Lane, Mark entered his house, ready to face whatever challenges lay ahead. Their journey had just begun, and like the flickering lights of a Christmas tree, Mark's hope burned bright, destined to illuminate the path towards a harmonious and welcoming community on Ravenscroft Lane.

CHAPTER 2

STUPID & STUPIDER

Candy and Shirley Garrison stood side by side in their new bedroom, their belongings scattered haphazardly throughout the space. While Shirley, the younger of the two sisters, meticulously organized her self-help books and desk supplies, Candy flitted around the room with a carefree energy, distracted by the colourful decorations and mesmerized by her own reflection in the mirror.

"Shirley, do you think this shade of pink matches my hair?" Candy asked, holding up a pillowcase adorned with vibrant roses.

Shirley sighed; her eyes fixed on the mountain of textbooks she was unpacking. "Candy, we have been through this. Candy, your hair is blonde, not pink."

Candy blinked at her sister; her blue eyes filled with playful confusion. "Oh, right! Silly me, I always mix things up. But seriously, how cool would it be if I had pink hair?"

Shaking her head with an exasperated smile, Shirley replied, "Candy, you're perfect just the way you are. And besides, you'll always be my lovable, if slightly ditzy, big sister."

Candy giggled and twirled around the room, a trail of laughter trailing behind her. "Well, at least I bring the entertainment factor, right?"

Shirley chuckled and reached over to tousle Candy's hair gently. "That you do, Candy. That you do."

As the girls continued to unpack and settle into their new surroundings, they could not help but feel a mixture of excitement and trepidation. The move to Ravenscroft Lane meant a fresh start. School life had been hard since Candy her sister had repeated two years placing herself in Year 12 with Shirley. Finally, both sisters left behind the judgmental classmates who had never understood their failures of not being lucky enough to pass a test unlike the brains who advance 3 years at school.

Within this new neighbourhood, the sisters hoped to find a sense of belonging, each in their own unique way. Shirley longed for personal development and deep connections, while Candy simply wanted to be loved and accepted for who she was, blonde hair and all.

Candy, ever the social butterfly, effortlessly befriended the neighbourhood boys, believing it was her contagious laughter and easy-going nature drawing them in like moths to a flame. She quickly referred to herself as the girl with the infectious smile, her joyfulness bringing life and vibrancy to Ravenscroft Lane.

Shirley, on the other hand, sought solace in a staff room at her father's place of employment. Her nose buried in Dr Seuss books and notepad in hand. She found comfort in the silence of the nursing home and the feeling of knowledge seeping into her very being. It was here that she discovered the true power of her sub-normal intellect and the potential it held.

Later that Sunday evening the neon lights flickered, casting a vibrant glow on the bustling arcade as Candy and her friends entered. Excitement bubbled within her, fuelled by the prospect of new friendships and the chance to make lasting memories on this fateful night. Their laughter filled the room as they maneuverer between the flashing screens and the melodic sounds of arcade games.

Candy's heart skipped a beat as she reached the counter and prepared to register for the first time. Standing behind the register was a dirty old man with the kind of eyes that require a restraining order. Leaning against the counter with a mischievous grin on his face.

"ID, please," he requested, stretching out his hand expectantly.

Candy fumbled in her purse, her hand curiously gripping onto her ID card. She hesitated for a moment, feeling a pang of self-consciousness, knowing that she was older than her friends who were eagerly awaiting.

"Grade 12, huh? Looks like the new girl is a bit old for high school, aren't ya?" the creepy man remarked, amusement dancing in his eyes as he glanced creepily between Candy and her ID.

A blush crept onto Candy's cheeks as she handed over her ID, aware that her situation might seem unconventional. "Yeah, I had to repeat a grade.

Long story," she managed to say, hoping her explanation would satisfy his curiosity.

The dirty old man chuckled, his laughter filling the arcade. "It is all good. In this place being nineteen does not matter. Have fun tonight, new girl."

Candy's uncertainty melted away not understanding his sarcastic response. She realized that her age, her journey, and her experiences were unique, but they only added to the richness of her story. With newfound confidence, she accepted her ID back and stepped into the arcade, ready to embrace the joyful chaos that awaited her.

Throughout the afternoon, Candy, and her friends, with their shared laughter and competitive spirit, forged a bond that went beyond age or social expectations. The initial moments of amusement at Candy's situation melted away, replaced by genuine camaraderie and the thrill of friendly competition. As they played game after game, Candy's vivacious spirit and quick wit provided endless entertainment. Her friends, despite their initial surprise, soon realized that Candy's age was inconsequential in the grand tapestry of their friendship.

The dirty old man at the register, witnessing the genuine connection between Candy and her friends, could not help but be intrigued by her presence.

"I hope you had a blast, new girl," he said, addressing Candy with a pathetic squeak in his voice.

Candy grinned back, feeling a sense of acceptance, and belonging in this unexpected encounter. "Thanks, arcade man. This was an amazing evening! I cannot wait to start school tomorrow and see what other adventures await."

"No need for that kind of discussion. How about I use my tag to try you to win points on the dance floor?" Candy grimaced not seeing a dance floor anywhere. "Over here he pointed to a dance machine. "Step on the arrows of the floor as it shows on the screen and the sexier the dance moves the more points you earn."

Determined to spread holiday cheer through her lively moves, she stepped onto the dance platform, ready to captivate the dirty old man with her unique style. Flicking through the Christmas song list she noticed her favourite Christmas song. "Showbiz Christmas by Mr. Showbiz," Candy shouted pointing her finger toward the celling. Little did Candy understand she put the game on for two players thinking she had to utilise both platforms.

As the song "Showbiz Christmas" blared through the speakers, Candy's body moved in perfect sync with the rhythm, her energy radiating from every pore. With each well-coordinated dance move, she astonished the surrounding students, their eyes widening in disbelief at her skill, enthusiasm and egotistical song while singing poorly. "She is playing on two player and insane mode," shouted one of her male friends.

Candy sang beautifully, "Christmas eve at a Showbiz party and everyone looks the same, hello. I go around calling everybody sweety because I do not even know their name."

More boys gathered to witness her dance pulling out their smart phones. Candy's intricate footwork and fluid motions elicited gasps of awe and whispers of disbelief. Some parents caught off guard by her electrifying performance. Few mothers covered their children's eyes or used distraction strategies.

But despite the mix of reactions, Candy remained unfazed, lost in the joy of the music and the freedom of expression. She knew she was different, and she had embraced that difference long ago. Her vibrant spirit refused to be contained, especially during the festive season when joy and merriment were meant to be shared with abandon.

Noticing her two scores were not placing her at the top and sweating she began dancing more expressively as she removed her winter warmers. Parents inside a function room gasped covering the eyes of the boys at Johnathn's Bar mitzvah. Believing that one score was for her foot work and the other for the rest of her body seen in the reflection she wanted two first places for the song record.

Singing louder as more people gathered cheering for Candy. "S is for Sleighride, H is for Heaven." Candy banged her feet harder since not knowing the lyrics for that part of the song. "Showbiz is the business this Christmas." Then in an epic jump she grabbed the railing pushing her feet to the air as her skirt dropped. Thinking she was being sexy hearing everyone gasped shock. Little did she know her underwear revealed diamond-shaped skid marks.

"You totally killed it, Candy!" one of her friends exclaimed, grinning from ear to ear.

Candy laughed, the adrenaline still coursing through her veins. "Thanks, guys! I just wanted to bring some festive energy and spread the holiday spirit. I went all out!"

As the evening continued, Candy's infectious joy and fearless ability to be herself melted away any lingering judgment.

*   *   *

The sun rose, casting a golden glow over Ravenscroft Lane on Candy and Shirley's first day of school. Excitement mixed with anticipation as the sisters prepared themselves for the brand-new adventure that awaited them within the walls of their new school.

Clutching their backpacks tightly wearing what clothes feel best since this school did not require uniforms, they walked hand in hand towards the bustling corridors, ready to face the unknown. As they entered the school building, Candy spotted a group of students huddled together, laughing, and whispering. Curiosity piqued; she approached the group with Shirley trailing shyly behind.

Giggles erupted from the group as they took turns passing around a photo on their phones. Candy's heart skipped a beat as she caught a glimpse of the image—an unfortunate moment captured in time. It was a picture of her, mid-handstand on a steel pipe, revealing her colourful underwear adorned with diamond-shaped skid marks.

Embarrassment washed over Candy like an icy wave, while Shirley's face flushed with mortification. They had hoped for a fresh start, but it seemed that their first day of school would be marred by an unforgettable incident.

Candy felt a mix of anger and vulnerability rise within her, but she refused to let it overwhelm her spirit. Taking a deep breath, she approached the group, her voice steady but resolute.

"Hey, guys. I see you found this interesting photo. Yep, that is me, embracing the sheer joy of life without a care in the world," she said, a hint of defiance in her tone.

The students looked at her, their laughter subsiding as they registered her unwavering confidence. One of them, a girl with kind eyes, spoke up hesitantly, "we didn't mean to embarrass you, Candy. It just circulated around the school, and, well, you know how gossip spreads."

Candy smiled, "I get it. Gossip spreads just like when your Daddy spreads my legs to eat my cookie?"

The boy was embarrassed believing her insult. "From now on, let us spread kindness and understanding instead of laughing at each other's misfortunes. Life is too short to dwell on embarrassing moments."

The group nodded slowly, believing truth about the girl's father in Candy's words. In that moment, a shift occurred—a collective realisation that kindness and empathy were far more powerful than judgment. As the day unfolded, Candy's image gradually transformed from the girl caught in an embarrassing photo to someone known for her vibrant spirit and unwavering self-assurance. The incident became a catalyst for growth, for her and for the people she encountered.

Candy had no idea that Shirly was embarrassed to be seen around her toxic positivity. Together, the sisters navigated the highs and lows of their new school, bolstered by their unbreakable bond and the genuine connections they forged along the way.

Candy had an idea. Going alone into the teacher's bathroom she searched for a highlighter. Only finding a green highlighter she continued with her cunning plan while Shirly waited for her.

As the bell rang, signalling the end of lunch time and the beginning of the next period, Shirley felt a mix of anticipation and nervousness ripple through her veins. She had found solace in the familiarity of her textbooks and the comfort of the classroom, but the social dynamics of the school remained uncharted territory.

Candy stood in front of the teachers' bathroom, a mischievous twinkle in her eyes as she dangled a bright green highlighter in her hand. Shock coursed through Shirley's veins at the audacity of Candy's actions. While she admired her sister's ability to embrace individuality, she could not help but worry about the consequences this bold act might have on Candy's reputation, and by extension, their own social standing.

As the bell for the next class echoed through the hallways, Shirley mustered up her courage, determined to intervene before it was too late. She approached Candy, her voice laced with concern and urgency.

"Candy, what are you doing? Is this really the best time to draw attention to ourselves?" Shirley whispered, her eyes glancing nervously at their peers passing by.

Candy turned to her, a defiant smile playing on her lips. "Shirley, remember what we spoke about, embracing who we are? Well, this is me embracing my uniqueness. I refuse to conform to others' expectations or let fear hold me back."

Shirley sighed, her worry giving way to a spark of understanding. She realized that Candy's actions were a testament to her unwavering spirit, and that beneath her carefree exterior, she possessed a strength and wisdom that Shirley admired.

Taking a deep breath, Shirley made a conscious choice to stand in solidarity with her sister. She remembered the challenges they had overcome together, and the unspoken pact they had made to support one another no matter what.

With a newfound sense of determination and conviction, Shirley squared her shoulders and smiled at Candy. "Alright then, let us own this. Embrace our uniqueness and prove that we can be ourselves without fear or shame."

The sisters noticed a Christmas flyer on a notice board outside Dr. Tracy Jenolan's life skills class at Gwenvale High advertising a new award for the most decorative street in Gwenvale region. Grabbing the flyer, the two sisters held their heads high despite the whispers and curious glances that followed them. They became beacons of self-assurance, reminding their peers that conforming to societal norms was not the only pathway to happiness and acceptance. Setting a new trend to blonde students alike as the school day ended, a new trend of highlighter hairstyles was now part of a new Christmas fashion.

In this newfound landscape of acceptance, Candy and Shirley forged bonds with classmates who valued their authenticity and respected their choices. They formed friendships grounded in mutual respect, where each person's quirks and idiosyncrasies were celebrated rather than stigmatized.

"Hello Ms, my name is Candy, I am the one with special needs," Candy introduced cheerfully while her teacher Dr. Tracy Jenolon paused for a few seconds before introducing herself.

Side by side, they grew stronger and inspired others to embrace their own individuality, creating a vibrant community that celebrated the kaleidoscope of differences that made them who they were—two sisters who found strength and wisdom in the most unlikely of moments, lighting up the path for others to do the same. The sisters began to think the same could be achieved on Ravenscroft Lane.

CHAPTER 3

ASSHOLES UNITE

As the snowflakes fell gracefully from the sky, blanketing Ravenscroft Lane in a pristine layer of white, Mark and Melissa ran across the street returning home. "Emergency meeting," Mark called out ringing his Christmas bell. Candy and Shirley came downstairs confused by their fathers more than unusual behaviour. "I wanted to discuss an idea that had been brewing in my mind since the unforgettable street meeting."

The family of four sat around waiting for Mark to initiate proceedings. "Mr. Fredrickson clearly does not want to celebrate Christmas let alone decorate his home. So, I need us to brainstorm ideas to help this man in a way that includes him in the festivities for the Christmas lights competition. Since the competition means so much to this community.

"Mark but what about our Advent family traditions. Promise me that this Christmas season is not going to get out of hand like the Christmas at your workplace three years ago," Melissa asked concerned.

Candy, always full of surprises, sat on the couch, her eyes shining with anticipation. She was below average in all her classes, yet she had a knack for seeing connections where others overlooked them, and her life skills class had sparked an idea within her curious mind.

"I have an idea," Candy exclaimed, a mischievous smile playing on her lips. "What if we interview people from our street, school and your workplace, Mom? We can give them a chance to tell their stories and see if there's common ground among us. It could be fascinating!"

Mark smiled, "I have loads of stories in my workplace as well and heck, Shirley can work on this as a book in the life skills class and get your teacher to publish it."

"Eww, old people dad. You know as a Registered Nurse, you could have him committed to your workplace and we could decorate his house in his absence," Candy explained then concerning thoughts could be seen expressively on her face.

Melissa and Shirley exchanged intrigued glances. The idea of understanding their peers on a deeper level resonated with their own desires for connection and unity. Mark nodded, recognizing the potential impact of Candy's idea. "That's a remarkable suggestion, sweetheart. It could help us bridge any gaps and find the common threads that tie us together. Let us start by reaching out to our neighbours and scheduling these interviews."

With renewed excitement, Mark, Melissa, Candy, and Shirley set out to bring their idea to life. They knocked on doors, explaining their vision and inviting their neighbours to share their stories and experience. News spread quickly on Ravenscroft Lane, and soon, residents eagerly signed up to participate in the interviews. People were longing to be heard and understood, and the opportunity to connect with their neighbours captivated their hearts.

As the Garrison family conducted the interviews that evening, they witnessed the power of authentic conversations. Neighbors shared tales of good, bad, ugly and miracles, discovering common ground beneath the surface of their differences. Families who had once lived parallel lives found themselves drawn together by shared experiences. They laughed, cried, and empathized with one another, their stories melting away barriers, fostering a newfound sense of compassion, and understanding.

*   *   *

The holiday season had arrived in full splendour on Ravenscroft Lane, and with it came the age-old tradition of the Christmas decoration competition. However, this year, there was a twist. The head judge announced that participation would require every single household on the street to join in the festivities keeping consistency in a selected theme. The news spread quickly, and with it came a renewed sense of excitement and anticipation.

Tom Henderson, a dedicated member of Ravenscroft Lane, saw the competition as an opportunity to bring his neighbours together in a way they had never experienced before. He decided to host a street meeting in his living room, inviting all 30 houses on Ravenscroft Lane to discuss the competition.

Mark Garrison, a kind-hearted and enthusiastic individual, had recently become a familiar face in the neighbourhood. He was thrilled and nervous when Tom's invitation arrived, and he eagerly prepared himself for the gathering.

As the residents filled Tom's living room, a festive atmosphere blanketed the space. The twinkling lights from the Christmas tree reflected in their excited eyes. Tom's wife, Sarah, and their 14-year-old son, Patrick, welcomed each guest with warm smiles and cups of steaming hot cocoa.

After heartfelt introductions and mingling, Tom stood before the group confused to the shirt that Mark and his wife Melissa were wearing. "What type of print do you have on your shirts?" Tom raised an eyebrow surprised. "It is a Garrison family tradition to celebrate life day every seventeenth of November. Heck, we get out of work to celebrate each year."

"Life day," Tom asked puzzled. Melissa stood up explaining to everyone. "Life day is Christmas for our friends in a galaxy far-far away. After the meeting we are going to watch the Star Wars Holiday Special if anyone wants to join us."

Simultaneously every snapped, "No."

After a moment of awkward silence Tom initiated the meeting. "Thank you all for joining me tonight as we embark on a journey to unite our street in the spirit of Christmas. As you know, the competition requires the participation of every household on Ravenscroft Lane. However, we are missing a crucial member, Mr. Fredericks."

The mention of Mr. Fredericks brought a hushed silence over the room. Mr. Fredericks was notorious for his resistance to community events. Mark remembered his encounter with Mr. Fredericks understanding the challenge ahead. But he believed that this competition would not only bring joy and camaraderie to the street but might also shine a light on the goodness in Mr. Fredericks' heart.

"Being new to the area, perhaps I could initiate conversations with Mr. Fredericks," Mark spoke up, his voice confident yet gentle. "He wants to be a part of this community and being elderly, I know the electrical bill for running Christmas lights is difficult. We need to approach him with compassion, understanding, see things from his point of view and an offer him an invitation that he cannot refuse."

Tom nodded, appreciating Mark's insight. "You're right, Mark. Let us gather some creative ideas for the Christmas decorations and formulate a plan to approach Mr. Fredericks together."

The room quickly filled with lively discussions and inventive suggestions. The residents brainstormed ideas that would capture Mr. Fredericks' interest and make him feel valued as part of the street. They wanted him to see the competition as an opportunity for connection, rather than an intrusion. With a plan in place and the excitement of their shared mission fuelling their spirits, Mark joined Tom and a group of neighbours as they walked down the street to Mr. Fredericks' house.

They knocked on the door, nerves and hope intertwined within their hearts. When Mr. Fredericks opened the door, his face etched with curiosity, they saw a rare glimmer of anticipation in his eyes. Tom, Mark, and their neighbours spoke with sincerity, explaining their vision for the competition and how important it was for the entire street to come together. They emphasized the opportunity for connection and community building, and the shared joy that would come from participating in a unified effort.

For a moment, Mr. Fredericks seemed lost in thought. The weight of years of seclusion lifted slightly as he acted sarcastically pretending that their words were permeating his heart. "Oh, my aching heart. I suppose...it would not hurt to try it," Mr. Fredericks finally replied, a faint smile gracing his lips.

Cheers erupted from the group; their excitement contagious. They left Mr. Fredericks' porch with a newfound sense of triumph, thinking that their perseverance and unity had brought them one step closer to creating the most memorable Christmas celebration Ravenscroft Lane had ever seen.

"Clearly you do not understand sarcasm. Keep Christmas Traditions to yourself and I will keep my Christmas traditions to myself." Tom interrupted, "but you don't keep any Christmas traditions."

Despite their continuous efforts to convince him to participate in the Christmas decoration competition, he remained resistant.

"Mr. Fredricks would you please reconsider. You do not have to put any efforts into decorating your house. Neighbours are willing to run extension leads to your home and compensate you for any electricity costs," Tom Henderson announced loudly as forty people stood around.

"I do not celebrate Christmas. You ask for decades and persist that I celebrate this day," Mr. Fredricks yelled irately from the patio. As snow fell softly around them, transforming the landscape into a winter wonderland, the negotiation reached a climactic moment as the neighbours began carolling excessively.

Frustration filled the chilly air as Mr. Fredericks stood his ground, his stubbornness unyielding. But fate had a different plan in store. As tensions rose from the carollers, Mr. Fredericks rushed outside with a baseball bat.

"Get lost," Mr. Fredricks swung his bat around wildly to push carollers away without intentions to hit. "I said get lost," Mr. Fredricks yelled as he suddenly overextended his upward swing losing his footing on the icy ground, causing him to slip and fall with a thud. His neighbours rushed to his side. Their faces read guilt and confusion, as Tom Henderson the neighbourhood busybody called an ambulance to tend to his injuries.

Amid the chaos, as Mr. Fredericks was carefully loaded onto the ambulance, a profound realization washed over the hearts of those around him. They realised that the spirit of togetherness that had been ignited on Ravenscroft Lane was about more than just Christmas decorations—it was about caring for one another, even during disagreements.

As the ambulance drove away, its flashing lights casting a somber glow, the residents of Ravenscroft Lane huddled close together, their breaths visible in the wintry air. The incident had served as a stark reminder of the fragile nature of life and the importance of fostering connections and unity within their community.

The falling snowflakes, once a gentle backdrop, began to intensify, turning into a snowfall that seemed to mirror the emotions swirling around Ravenscroft Lane. The weight of the situation hung in the air, prompting neighbours to reflect on their own actions, pledging to approach their relationships with more kindness and understanding.

*　*　*

Tom and the other neighbours took turns checking on Mr. Fredericks at the hospital, offering support and assistance to his family in his absence. The incident became a catalyst for compassion, as they recognized that their true strength lay in their ability to come together, regardless of differences or disagreements. Little did Mr. Fredricks realise that one of his neighbours is a doctor who purposely miss diagnosed him as unable to care for himself. Mr. Fredricks received temporary accommodation at Gwenvalle Nursing home where Mark Garrison worked. And so, on that wintry day, as the snow continued to fall, the residents of Ravenscroft Lane discovered that true community was not born from mere holly and garlands, but from empathy, connection, and a commitment to embracing one another's stories, even when it seemed impossible. In the days that followed, the Garrisons continued their interviews, framing them within the context of the snowstorm and Mr. Fredericks' accident. They saw their neighbours rally around one another, offering help with snow removal, providing warm meals, and reaching out with heartfelt compassion.

As the final flakes settled on the lane, changing the landscape into a serene winter scene, Ravenscroft Lane stood as a testament to the resilience and strength that can be found within a community that truly seeks to understand each other. They understood that the true essence of the competition lay not in winning, but in the bond, they had formed—a bond that stemmed from interviews, shared stories, and the snowfall that brought them closer together on Ravenscroft Lane.

*　*　*

Tom Henderson, an overweight man with a forceful heart full of holiday cheer, stood outside his house on Ravenscroft Lane with his wife, Sarah, and their son, Patrick. Excitement filled the air as the family and neighbours prepared to decorate Mr. Fredricks home for the Christmas season. Little did they know that their decorating venture would be filled with unexpected mishaps and comical situations.

Tom Henderson began his speech on the front porch of Mr. Fredricks house. "Alright gentlemen, posh women, and children of all ages. Ravenscroft Lane has rules, and we expect everyone to follow them. For us to win this year's ultimate prize we must stick together like flies to a pile of cow dung. The residents of Frecklington street have stuck to a Frosty the snowman theme and as for our rivals the Baptist Christians have a nativity theme outside each house on Catilyn Street. But if we stick together and we all pitch in our labour, time, resources, and some money for Santa to give candy canes to pedestrians and automobile drivers coming to our neighbourhood then I am as certain as a nutcracker, that this year we will crack many nuts."

Someone shouted from the crowd. "Peter Richardson and his friends from the Nankin City Drama Society have displayed a Star Wars Christmas theme on Willow Street." Tom grimaced, "who shouted out that absurd statement." Tom walked through the crowd as they stepped aside slowly. Standing alone waving over enthusiastically was a man in his forties. "Andrew, you do not even live in this neighbourhood. Please leave your references aside and let us get to work."

Tom thought it was best to get started grabbing the first string of lights. As Tom climbed up the ladder to hang the first string of lights, a mischievous squirrel running along the guttering startled him, causing him to lose his balance and tumble backward. Falling off the ladder he crashed with a mighty thud leaving a crater where he landed on his buttock. Sarah, trying to untangle the Christmas lights after Tom's fall. Accidentally getting her foot caught in the wire, causing her to trip and fall into a pile of snow.

Meanwhile, Patrick is carrying a box of ornaments noticing Candy riding her bike and wearing a mini skirt despite the winter season. "Sport she is a bit too old for you. A lady like that would break your adolescent heart and make a grown man cry," stated the dirty old neighbour with his pencil trimmed mustacho who worked at the arcade. Patrick commented, "She was held back two years and thankfully I moved up three years in school."

"If you want to impress a girl like that stick a large ornament down your pants," said the dirty old man.

Patrick accidentally dropped the box of ornaments causing glitter and shatterproof balls to spill everywhere, creating a sparkling mess. Another man set up the inflatable Santa Claus decoration that suddenly came to life before they were ready, knocking into the mailbox and causing it to topple over.

Tom delegated the Christmas light duty to another man while taking on a simpler task. While attempting to hang a wreath on the front door, Tom accidentally hooked his sweater onto a nail, getting himself stuck and requiring Sarah's assistance to free him. As Michelle was setting up their spare life-size nativity scene, a strong gust of wind blew through, knocking over several figurines and causing them to shatter in pieces across the yard.

"Oh, piss it," Melissa cursed kicking one of the heads accidentally knocking over a bucket of silver tinsel, sending it cascading down Ravenscroft Lane.

Patrick noticed an opportunity to play his smooth moves on Candy walking toward her almost looking misguided under the influence of alcoholic eggnog. Neighbours gasped not realising that Patrick not only stuck an ornament in his undies, but he stuck it at the rear end. "Is it just me or has Candy come early this Christmas season?" Candy laughed at Patrick as a curious cat sneaked into the middle of their decorating chaos and proceeded to bat at ornaments and tangle itself scratching Candy as Patrick tried helplessly to remove the excess tinsel.

Just as Tom finished arranging a row of decorative candy canes along the pathway, a mischievous neighbourhood dog raced by and snapped them up running down Ravenscroft Lane. "No, no, no," Tom panicked chasing the dog.

Shirley carefully positioned the reindeer lawn decorations. Reaching to hang a decorative bell, accidentally swatted at a wasp, resulting in a small commotion and a hasty retreat. One of the neighbours untangled the string of lights and was ready to succeed where Tom had failed. Pulling out his small mallet hammer he banged in the first nail so hard that he smashed through the guttering.

To his surprise he shouted, "get back." Tom failing to hang a decorative wreath stepped out to see what the commotion was. The guttering fell by his feet. In a moment of shock, he screamed like a girl giving Sarah a sudden fright who was positioning a Santa Claus decoration on the roof. She stumbled tapping her feet into the roof trying to keep her balance. Once still she took a much-needed deep breath. Then in a moment of distraction witnessing the chaos down below she stepped on a patch of ice. Cursing and sliding down the slope she landed by Michelle.

Michelle was holding a ladder for another neighbour to get onto the roof while accidentally stepping on a sharp broken garden gnome. Kicking it in a fit of rage sending it flying through the patio window shooting past two other neighbours' kids. Sarah decided to go for a change of pace just like her husband Tom. Hanging ornaments on a tree to the side of the house. No ladder needed just patience. In a moment of boredom, she accidentally dropped a box causing the ornaments to shatter against a rock that she did not notice before.

In a moment of frustration Candy shouted several suggestions. "Enough, this house is old and falling apart. This dork made a mess, the roof is falling apart, and you know the classic saying.

IT'S ONLY GOING TO GET WORSE!"

"What do you propose?" Tom asked curiously then glared shocked to see his son Patrick standing closet to Candy.

"How about a new theme?"

Gossiping all around waiting for her to suggest something. "The Baptists put on a hell house for Halloween to touch on various issues like poofters burning in Hell and raw meat used to represent an abortion. So let us do a hell house theme this year of our own seen the house interior is sturdier than the exterior."

Blank stares towards Candy as no one understands what she is saying. "This year's theme: The Asshole Who Didn't Want to Celebrate Christmas."

Laughter could be heard all around as everyone gathered. Patrick conveniently provided Candy a step ladder so she may present a speech the whole neighbourhood would remember.

"The theme consists of everyone celebrating Christmas as a neighbourhood. Then in this Hell House we provide a tour. Instead of bedroom two consisting of what I previously mentioned. We give a representation of Ebenezer Scrooge meets the Ghost of Christmas past reflecting on an asshole and the girl who got away."

Candy began her announcement fully enjoying the attention she was receiving. "Oh, can I audition for The Ghost of Christmas Present?" Tom Garrison offered eagerly.

Candy paused as she thought of some ideas. "I can book out the classroom at school and host auditions. I mean Shirley can organise and we can take notes from your stories to find the true meaning of Christmas and turn it into a book."

CHAPTER 4

TRAPPED IN A PURGATORY HOME

Mark Garrison entered the sterile, white-walled room of the nursing home, his heart heavy with concern for Mr. Fredericks. The sight of the elderly man lying in bed, his face etched with pain, sent a pang of sympathy coursing through Mark's veins. He approached the bedside, careful not to disturb his fragile state.

"Mr. Fredericks," Mark said gently, his voice conveying both empathy and determination. "I have just spoken with the doctors. They have diagnosed you with a hairline fracture on your hip and a dislocated shoulder. It will take time, but you will heal." Mr. Fredericks' eyes met Mark is, a mixture of disbelief and anger reflecting in them. Slowly, the reality of his situation began to set in. Mark understood the difficult road Mr. Fredericks would face on the path to recovery, but he was determined to be a source of support during this challenging time since he has not declared any next to kin.

"The nurse will assist you with general observations and help with any necessary tasks, such as taking your shower," Mark continued, his tone gentle yet firm. "I know it might be difficult, but personal hygiene is important. It has been a week since your last shower and despite your rights you need to let us help you so, please help us to help you."

"Stop right there. Something tells me that you could go in circles all day and I see that you would," Mr. Fredricks groaned.

Reluctance flickered across Mr. Fredericks' face, his pride momentarily clashing with the practicality of Mark's words. "I have not had a shower in months. I do not need one." Mark glanced towards the nurse, who stood nearby, ready to provide support and guidance. "Ms. Henzler here will assist you with your observations. She will make sure you are as comfortable as possible. Do not hesitate to ask for any additional help you may need," Mark gave a cheeky wink.

Mrs. Henzler smiled warmly at Mr. Fredericks, her gentle presence offering reassurance in the unfamiliar environment. She understood the importance of respecting his dignity and autonomy, even in times of vulnerability. "Now," Mark continued, "the nurse will prompt you to make your bed. And I have a feeling we could use a hand from our male nurse, who happens to be quite skilled in the art of bed-making," Mark sounded sarcastic knowing his coworker was useless at basic domestic duties that a seven-year-old could do.

With a twinkle in his eye, Mark gestured towards the male nurse, who stood nearby, his arms crossed, belying his confidence in his abilities. Despite the gravity of the situation, a chuckle escaped Mark's lips, bringing a momentary lightness to the room.

The male nurse stepped forward, grinning at the sight of Mr. Fredericks making rude hand gestures. "Alright, Mr. Fredericks, let us get that bed in shape. I do not want to brag, but Mrs. Henzler's bed-making skills are legendary."

As Mark prepared his equipment to leave the room, he turned to Mr. Fredericks one final time. "Take your time and allow yourself to heal, Mr. Fredericks. We will be here to support you every step of the way. Ravenscroft Lane is more than just a street—it is a community that cares."

With those words, Mark exited the room, leaving Mr. Fredericks to begin his journey of healing and recovery surrounded by the attention and care he so desperately needed. "My name is Andrew, and I will help you in the shower while Mrs. Henzler makes your bed."

"Why can't she give me the shower?" Mr. Fredricks asked desperately. "If you saw my bed making skills you would certainly laugh," Andrew reassured him laughing at his inabilities. Mr Fredricks belted out a verse singing, "love is in the air," as he was directed to the shower.

* * *

Lunchtime came around quickly. Mr. Fredericks sat in his wheelchair, surrounded by a lively group of fellow residents in the dining room. They chatted away, their voices overlapping as laughter filled the air. It was an eclectic mix of personalities, each with their own unique story to tell.

Curiosity got the better of Mr. Fredericks, and with a mischievous twinkle in his eye, he turned to the woman and man sitting at the same table. "So," he began, his voice tinged with humour. "What are you two in for? I feel like we are in some sort of prison here."

The woman, who introduced herself as Miss Patterson, chuckled and leaned in closer. "Well, Mr. Fredericks, I am here for my exceptional talent for misplacing my keys, phone, and anything else I deem important. They decided it was safer for everyone if I had round-the-clock supervision."

A burst of laughter erupted from the table, the residents finding humour in the relatability of Mrs. Patterson's forgetfulness. Mr. Fredericks could not help but join in, his spirits lifting as he connected with these newfound companions.

The man, who introduced himself as Mr. Jenkins, chuckled and replied, "Ah, well, I am here because my family believes I have an uncanny ability to cause chaos with even the simplest of household objects. My expertise in turning a perfectly functional toaster into a flaming ball of fire became too much for them to handle. Same said for the kitchen staff here. Each time they burn toast the Nankin Emergency Volunteers come since there are not enough fire brigade to deal with burned toast."

Ms Patterson interrupted, "my family sent me here after my handbag caught flames and burned my house down." Mr Fredricks Grimaced, "how the hell do you burn a house down from a handbag?"

Ms Patterson shrugged as the table erupted in uproarious laughter, the image of a toaster or handbag going up in flames painting a comical picture in their minds. Mr. Fredericks found solace in the camaraderie and shared experiences, realizing that even in the most unexpected places, friendships could be forged.

As the laughter subsided, the male nurse, with a wink and a grin, approached the table, holding a tray of finger food entrees. Each portion sported a small, decorative umbrella that added a touch of whimsy to the food.

"Alright, ladies and gentlemen, finger foods for everyone!" the male nurse proclaimed, his enthusiasm infectious. He skilfully distributed the entrees, carefully placing the whimsical umbrella decorations on each plate. Mr. Fredericks could not resist a sarcastic remark, his sense of humour shining through. "Well, I must admit, I have never had the pleasure of dining with an umbrella before. How fancy of you, good sir."

The male nurse chuckled, clearly appreciating Mr. Fredericks' wit. "Why, Mr. Fredericks, we only provide the finest dining experience here. You will have to let us know if these umbrellas elevate your culinary journey or a creative Christmas hat for our first of December Christmas Party."

Miss Patterson smiled, "so can the nursing home afford to take us out this year to see the Christmas lights or is it just non-existent?"

"I believe that the registered nurse Mark has a plan up his sleeve this year."

Mr Fredriks began an angry rant. "I hate Christmas, I had six mouths to feed, and my kids grew up fine without Christmas. This millennial generation grows up entitled for too much especially if there are more siblings in one household. Good luck to those having a white kid, black kid and throwing an Asian in there not knowing who the father is but may as well have them raised on technology not working hard like we did."

Miss Patterson laughed. "When I was your age, the meat was quail done," laughing at her pun. "Now kids expect mummy and daddy to put a duck inside a Turkey and a chicken inside the duck's rear end. Turducken," Mrs. Patterson began making several obscure noises.

Tears of laughter erupted once again, the residents joining Mr. Fredericks in his sarcastic delight. In that moment, the shared levity served as a balm for their souls, healing the wounds of confinement and establishing a sense of belonging in their unanticipated community.

Mark Garrison sat at the table for a moment. "Please share your stories. The good, bad, ugly and miracles of Christmas. I will make a genuine attempt to make this Christmas the best Christmas yet."

"Stop interrupting Mark and get back to work," snapped an overweight lady dishing up the main course.

* * *

Later that day Miss Paterson began telling Christmas stories from her past as Mark Garrison tended to her daily leg wound care. For a good Christmas story. A choir visits us several times per year singing songs of Christmas long forgotten. It takes me back to being the little girl by her loving father's side doing arts and crafts.

I remember a bad Christmas was being trapped in a cabin as a frightening blizzard came over. Trying to open a door and snow flowing inside. We were buried in with the electricity cut to the neighbourhood. Doing a reverse

Saint Nick on day seven, when I was in my twenties climbing up the well-used chimney. Covered head to toe in soot coughing all the way up. Once I reached the top, I noticed my husband opened the door stepping outside. One dreadful day did not mean all days ahead were bad being buried in snow. It also did not occur to me to look out the windows of the cabin in Gwenvale forest."

"Sounds like an adventure if you have enough supplies to get through the unforeseeable weather."

Ms Patterson grinned cheeky telling her next short story. "I was more distracted by my husband's sexual charisma that it was the birth of a new year. Now an ugly Christmas or as I like to call it... Christmas eve sales for retard bargain hunters. The local garden shop was selling everything from, concrete statues to Christmas dioramas that light up a winter wonderland spectacle all twenty percent off. Shopping violence like no other. Plants were grabbed by the leaves not the pot. Some adults managed to bring through their own customised trollies or as one wanker did. He walked in his Harley and side cart loading in expensive products to sit by his toddlers' feet. Considering that the bike could not fit through without patrons running back into the garden area as he gets served. Then the useless dickhead forgot his wallet to he had to put everything back. What was worse is his child being at constant risk and yet the garden shop would have no more than five customers at a time throughout the two-acre paradise."

Mark sighed, "shopping is my primary pet peeve for Christmas that is where I do all shopping in November. The way people behave certainly makes this season difficult for tolerate."

Ms Patterson continued to tell another story since Mark has nearly finished tending to her wounds.

"Finally good sir I have a true story about a Christmas miracle. My friend went through a custody battle and for years had limited access to his daughter. Court orders and false claims kept them apart. Now, the true meaning of Christmas is to enjoy the season. See here, for his one day per fortnight dragged out for years yet tutoring his son right from wrong. The reasons for divorce were financial as are many marriages today. He may not get to celebrate the day, but he celebrates the season while the mother puts all the Christmas chaos into one day. In seasons come and gone that girl now enjoys the whole season from December first till the new year. Enjoy this season to have a truly abundant life."

Mark began thinking to himself since he thought he enjoyed the whole season though he did not realise that he had unnecessary shopping pressures placed on his family. Realising selfishly from years passed his family enjoyed Christmas for his benefit more than their own.

CHAPTER 5

AUDITIONS & TRADITIONS

Candy and Shirley booked out the stage inside their life skills classroom at Gwenvale High since it was once a drama room.

Candy and Shirley are sitting at their teachers table, ready for auditions. Candy was flipping through pages looking at the pictures of each person auditioning since she could not read. "Alright, Shirley, we have got quite a few people coming in for auditions in our neighbourhood. We need to make sure we find the perfect cast for our Christmas hell house."

Shirley keenly responded, "Absolutely! We want people who can bring the story of Ebenezer Scrooge and the true meaning of Christmas to life. Let us make sure they understand the importance of this production taking the piss out of the community."

Candidates start walking in one by one as their name is called. "It is going to be tough to make final decisions. So many talented actors showed up."

Candy agreed, "I know, right? But we need to choose carefully. They need to be committed to delivering a powerful performance for seven nights straight."

Candidate one enters nervously clearing their throat, "Uh, hi! So, I am here to audition for the role of Ebenezer Scrooge." After a short pause she continued, "Sorry, got a little choked up there. Anyway, picture this: Ebenezer Scrooge, but with a twist that's not just gender flipped roles. He is a coupon-obsessed, penny-pinching miser. Instead of "Bah, humbug!" he says, "Bah, no discounts!""

Shirley locked her wrists forward then banged her hands together pulling a strange face, "Very... original interpretation. Next!"

"Candidate two is an African American teen. Entering energetically dressed as a skater wannabe rapper, "Hey there, ladies! I am here to audition for... ALL the roles! I will be the ghosts, the Cratchit family, Tiny Tim, Scrooge's lost love, and even that random caroller in the background." Holding his hand forward pausing for a moment. "And if time allows, I will throw in a tap-dancing reindeer too!"

"Wow, that is quite the range. How would you feel about playing Ebenezer Scrooge going through all four bedrooms and once final scene in the back yard looking at a tombstone in regret? Begging for a chance at redemption in a climax of climaxes."

"It is no problem to perform roles between rooms. Then afterwards I could get to know you better making love in each bedroom since the Grinch stole Christmas and you stole my heart." Candy reacted throwing her water bottle. "Asshole! You are on the naughty list."

He left hastily as candidate three was none other than Patrick entering timidly, clutching a stuffed animal. "Um... hi. So, I have prepared a dramatic interpretation of the iconic "God Bless Us, Everyone!" line. But, uh... I will be using my stuffed unicorn friend here to do the talking. Patrick starts doing a ventriloquist act with the stuffed animal.

Candy cringed struggling to keep a straight face. "Alright, interesting choice. We found our Tiny Tim." Patrick formally bowed running off stage.

Next is the dirty old neighbour with the pencil trimmed mustacho who works at the arcade. Wearing an oversized Christmas trench coat. "Hey, y'all! I am here to audition as Ebenezer Scrooge, but with a Southern twang. Picture this: Scrooge, the sassy Southern belle. Instead of saying "Bah, humbug!" I will say "Well, butter my biscuits!"

Opening one part of his trench coat it was clear that he was not wearing anything underneath as he twirled. He switched sides twirling around counterclockwise. Shirley tried to take a closer look unsure if her eyes had deceived her. Leaning forward she bumped a vase tipping over her teachers freshly cut roses. "Oops... you have been deflowered."

Candy grabbed a whistle and blew it hard making the creep run out the classroom door. Candy and Shirley, trying their best to contain their laughter. The auditions continue with more hilarity and surprises from the neighbourhood willing to make the best of the Hell House theme.

*   *   *

Candy and Shirley's father Mark accompanied by his wife Melissa are conversing with their neighbour, Mr. Tom Henderson, about their family's unique Christmas traditions. Mark could not help but feel a sense of accomplishment. He had successfully managed to create and implement 25 nights of family traditions, all inspired by the antique advent calendar that had been passed down for six generations. This festive journey had brought his family closer together and created countless unforgettable memories.

Now, there were only a few days left before December first and Mark could not wait to see what this year had install for them. Sitting in the cozy living room by the fireplace with the Henderson family, Mark watched his wife Melissa and their two daughters Candy and Shirley giggling and holding hands as they huddled over the advent calendar. Each night, they would eagerly open a new compartment, revealing a painted ruin they would embark upon the following day.

"Guess what, my loves?" Mark announced, capturing the girls' interest immediately. "After volunteering at the nursing home, I have a professional painter eager to paint our family portrait. As a way of welcoming us to the neighbourhood he has offered to paint our portrait for free."

Tom held his wife Sarah tightly. "You cannot go wrong with works of Geffory Widdy. He paints our portrait for our anniversary each year. Infact our anniversary is Christmas day since tradition needs to be shared, we who we love. Infact our Patrick was conceived Easter, and his birthday is boxing day. Just did not want to celebrate Christmas with his family."

"Well, we can't have everything we want," Mark in commented drawing the awkward attention away from Patrick. We have an antique wooden advent calendar to guide us forward each season with some variations for compromise."

Tom coughed hiding that he spat cookie crumbs into a mug before commenting. "Wowzers Mark. I thought we had Christmas problems, but it is clear to see your family traditions are just a way of getting out of work. Or that is what rumour says every year when I volunteer at the nursing home."

"I agree and disagree. Think of it as a way of making excuses to spend time together until my daughters go to college," Mark explained proudly.

"Just as a warning for Christmas eve. In this neighbourhood there is already an overweight sized man dressed as Santa giving presents to everyone," Sarah explained.

"Is it you Tom?"

"You would think it was me. No.... but whoever it is keeps tradition in this neighbourhood for all children and future generations to come. For now, we want you to see what a champion's house looks like for winning three years in a row and a total of ten wins."

Taking a closer look Mark realised he had stiff completion against the Hendersons. Noticing various pictures gave him ideas how to upstage the Hendersons determined to decorate better than Christmases past.

* * *

Meanwhile Patrick migrated to Candy and Shirley's bedroom where he showed them a YouTube video advertisement for a new anti-depressant drug for the Christmas season.

Attention all you holiday stress cases! Tired of feeling like Scrooge before his redemption? Say hello to "Mood Menders" - the anti-depression drug that will make you want to deck the halls and jingle all the way through the holiday season. Let us be real for a second, it is not all chestnuts roasting and sleigh bells ringing, sometimes it is only plain exhausting. And that's where Mood Menders comes in, a little pill that packs a big punch, like the naughty kid at family dinner who will not stop pulling on your stockings.

Do not worry, we will not judge you for needing a little extra help. Sometimes the stress of the holidays can make you want to hibernate like a Grinch, or worse... hangout with your in-law's way too long. Just pop a Mood Mender and you will feel like the star on top of the tree, or at least like you can tolerate your uncle's three-hour long story about his new tool shed. Think of Mood Menders as your own little Christmas miracle. You will be singing carols with the best of them, or at least humming "All I want for Christmas is a drink". With Mood Menders you can finally enjoy the holiday season, instead of grumpily pretending to like eggnog.

So, what are you waiting for? Whip out your credit card and say goodbye to feeling like a Scrooge and hello to being the Charlie Brown Christmas tree we all know and love. Just do not blame us if you start talking to your decorations, we warned you.

Shirley had an idea rush into her mind. "Patrick, we are trying to find a way to help Mr. Fredricks this Christmas season." Patrick interjected, "Its holiday season."

"What," Candy interrupted briskly. "My guidance Counceller tells me that in order to embrace diversity and not offend those who don't celebrate Christmas to feel alienated we should say Happy Holidays."

Candy reacted animatedly making use of inappropriate hand gestures and body language. "Childrens cartoons had a purpose to entertain and now children and preschoolers learn about sexual education as they are indoctrinated by politically correct narcissists creating a generation of children suffering from a gender identity crisis at mass scale. Now proving that homeschooling is not so bad. Long story short, f-bomb you its Merry Christmas."

Patrick laid back in the couch shocked to Candy's response, yet he believed everything she said. "How about we take a different approach," Shirley suggested. "Lay back and pretend you are in therapy and tell us both four stories. Good, bad ugly and miracles of Christmas so we may try and help Mr. Fredricks find his inner child's Christmas spirit."

Laying snuggly into the couch Patrick closed his eyes and began telling four stories. "A Christmas story before daddy's egotistical pride and mothers' greed for expensive possessions. It Twas the day after Christmas where rich folk donated their Christmas left over to the least fortunate."

Shirley took notes for her manuscript while prompting Patrick to continue.

"One day I noticed how grateful some were from homeless shelters to the nursing home. My parents pay wholesale from their business to use it as an opportunity to help others."

"It seems like their intentions are good so you cannot fault them for trying," Candy stated lovingly.

"One year an elderly man on a motorised bike wheelchair thingy said that Sarah woman is not so bright. I asked the man what was wrong. He said she gave presents to all the elderly, and I got socks for Christmas. I explained that was a nice gesture and intentions are to help others since government benefits are not enough. Then the man stated confused, I got no legs," everyone burst out laughing uncontrollably. Candy had tears in her eyes while Shirley softly tapped her notepad against her forehead.

"Now for a bad Christmas story. I woke up and my mother told me I was in a coma and missed the whole season showing me a Callender. Before she could reveal her humour, I was already dressed rushing for school. The school janitor laughed so hard I had to call an ambulance. I asked him what the number was for 911. Then he laughed harder that cause him pain and a two week stay in hospital."

Candy smirked, "I have repeated grades so at this stage its either learn what I need or become a janitor working for a surprising income or perhaps I should consider it," Candy began to ponder possibilities of employment.

"He has since recovered yet this is an ugly Christmas story. You know that guy in a trench coat who tried out for Hell House?"

Shirley put a finger in her mouth pretending to vomit. "Well, his name is Geffory Widdy, he is your neighbour, and you don't want to see his Instagram," Patrick shook his hands. Candy pulled up his Instagram gasping in shock. "He does what to paint a portrait? He wants to paint our family portrait!"

Shirley commented. "It can't be that bad and the upside is a free painting."

Candy turned her face away from her phone. "He uses Little Widdy as a paint brush." Patrick whimpered then continued to talk about Christmases past defecting the conversation.

"For my parents to stop telling the story about how I was conceived and born on boxing day. This is a story yet to happen but a miracle none the less." Little did Patrick know his father was listening in realising that he has been an asshole towards Patrick for being born the day after Christmas.

CHAPTER 6

HAVE

YOU

EVER

CONSIDERED

THAT

YOU

ARE

THE

ASSHOLE

WHO

DIDN'T

WANT

TO

CELEBRATE

CHRISTMAS?

CHAPTER 7

VOLUNTEERING

ark was eager to work the first of December since it was a Christmas party put on for all residents. Mark delegated staff and volunteers to transfer residents from the North, South, East and West wings of Gwenvalle Nursing Home to the central communal area where residents enjoyed a Christmas party with their families.

For the residents who refused to participate were expected to go to the West wing since staffing was tight to accommodate the party. Candy and Shirley volunteered their time with unusual intentions to help Mr. Fredrickson come to terms with his injuries, what the community are doing with his home and to find any spark of Christmas happiness while drafting a book in the process.

"Mr. Fredricks, there is a Christmas party held in the common room," Mark explained.

"Nah... Bugger that for a joke. I just want to watch crap on Tv and finish my coffee."

"Due to lack of registered staff needed for each unit the two choices are to join everyone at the Christmas party and for those who do not want to join need to go to the north unit. Since we are in the south unit and need to close it down for a few hours these are the only two options."

Mr. Fredricks continued to ignore. "I have not got time for this today. Either go to the North unit or join everyone at the Christmas party," Mark sounded firmer.

"Look I hate Christmas! How can anyone enjoy Christmas with two children to feed and now kids expect too much for the damn occasion each year."

Mark sighed heavily trying to remain calm.

"All year round this is the only couple of hours for compromise. Get through this and then you can do what you like while you are here. That is also until your signed off by the doctor to return home so for now you may as well try to enjoy yourself here."

Mr. Fredricks grabbed his wheelie walker then growled. "Fine I will go to the North unit. You know why I hate Christmas?"

Mark thought about how Shirley needed more information for stories for her book. Mr Fredricks would have some memorable stories to tell.

"Please, tell me more," Mark sounded sardonic with a hit of genuine empathy in his voice. Going into a passive aggressive monologue that made Mark wish someone else had to deal with Mr. Fredricks. Soon it would be made certain that they were opposite sides of the mental health Christmas spectrum.

"Ah, Christmas. The most joyous time of the year. Or so they say." Rolling his eyes not noticing Mark guide him past a slattered screen wall in the dining room. "Well, let me tell you something Nurse Dickhead. Christmas is nothing but a load of holly-jolly nonsense, wrapped up in sparkly shit paper that Povo folk hang out to dry."

"Now, Mr. Fredricks I understand you may not be a fan of Christmas, but some people enjoy the festive spirit. Once you return home perhaps, we could have you over for our Christmas eve party."

"Festive spirit? Bah! What is so festive about being crushed in a sea of holiday shoppers, desperately searching for the last roll of wrapping paper on the shelf? It is more pointless than the movie "Jingle All the Way" teaching children that love comes from consumerism."

Mark tried to shed some light on the subject yet struggled as Mr. Fredricks continued talking over the top of him. "Children? Oh, I have seen enough "Home Alone" marathons to know what joy children can bring during the holidays. Just a bunch of screaming, mischievous little devils causing chaos and leaving their parents to deal with the aftermath. No, sir, I will pass."

"Well, Christmas is not about kids and shopping. It is about spending time with loved ones."

"Loved ones, huh? Are you sure you have seen "Christmas Vacation"? Trust me, spending time with family during this season can be a recipe for disaster. Uncle Eddie emptying his RV's septic tank in the front yard? No thanks. And do not even get me started on those annoyingly cheery Christmas carols. It is enough to make me want to join the Grinch on Mount Crumpet! And that is another thing. Poor Grinch runs away, and no one thinks to look for an eight-year-old kid. He may just be less of an asshole than anyone in Whoville."

Mark paused taking time to process what Mr Fredricks was saying as his perspective changed ruining one of his most cherished Christmas movies.

"Well, Mr. Fredricks it seems like you have your reasons and you have seen some movies. Instead of watching a Christmas movie it would be best to share in more positive experiences."

Mark opened the door to the North unit letting Mr. Fredricks through. Inside was the dining room and simple kitchen where one lady was putting in another load into the dishwasher.

"Well, where the fuck is the Christmas party?" Puzzled for a moment Mark paused for a moment then explained. "This is the North Unit where you asked to go."

"I just could have stayed in my room."

* * *

Mark continued through various struggles wasting precious time. Meanwhile Candy and Shirley were happily volunteering at the Christmas party for sixty residents and eighty visitors of friends and families.

"Well, well, well if it isn't the Garrison sisters," Tom Henderson approached prancing as if he were on a toy horse.

"Hello Patricks dad," Candy said. "Please, we are all adults here. You can call me Tom," Mr. Tom Henderson explained.

"The nursing staff explained that they have bags of presents that are labelled according to table number. It is imperative that girls hand out one bag at a time per table to avoid confusion when passing out presents. But do not worry, each present has a sticker on it for individual names."

Candy offered, "Mr. Tom, where do we find these sacks?"

Tom Henderson sighed for a moment hearing his surname mistaken. "There is a small staff room out back. Nurses are currently busy preparing for the lunch ahead."

Candy and Shirley went out back. Little did they know between parents grabbing table number stands off their children and placing them at the wrong table. Candy grabbed sack number seven and progressed towards the table.

Candy kneaded beside Ms Patterson. "What is your name?" Ms Patterson answered lovingly, "Loretta and this is my daughter Carol, her husband Keith and their two children Rob and Ashely." Candy softened her voice sounding more degrading. "They are pretty names. My name is Candy and I have presents from Santa all the way from the North Pole." Instantly Loretta sighed looking at her family rolling her eyes. "I am Santas special little helper."

"Thats one way to call it," Ms Patterson mocked.

"Do we have an Ashley here?" An eager boy raised his hand. "Here, over here Mamm." Handing the young boy, a sparkling pink box his eyes squinted confused to see it. Opening the box, he burst into tears. "Why do I have a girl's toy?"

From another table a woman called out, "the presents probably got messed up." Quickly exchanging sacks Candy was able to hand out the presents as normal. "Here is a present for you Loretta. It is from Santa's workshop." Ms Patterson pointed to the label. "To Loretta from Loretta. I did not know if my family was going to asshole me this year since putting me in a prison for the elderly."

A crabby looking woman who looked as old as some of the residents grabbed Candy by the arm and took her out back while Loretta handed out the gifts from herself to her family. "Lesson number one is to never fully trust those you are trying to help. Lesson number two do not be such a useless spastic," said the crabby woman. "I am not spastic. I may be slow, but I am persistent to improve."

"Just give it up. The world has no time for idiots like you."

"Hey," shouted one of the bigger built male nurses. "Enough of that Rosealina. We are fortunate to have any help."

Rosealina stormed off in a hissy fit. "Hello, my name is Brett, and I am the one with special needs," he laughed.

Candy paused for a moment trying not to laugh, "hello Brett, my name is Candy and I to identify as special needs. As Dr. Tracy Jenolon says keep working on yourself."

Brett smiled, "I was in her class graduated twelve years ago but I did not worry about the high school reunion. What year did you graduate?"

Candy grimaced as she answered honestly, "I will graduate summer next year. I am nineteen years old struggling to pass mainstream education." Brett's eyes widened then he continued. "Math, English, and life skills class is what you need in the real world. Take a moment for yourself then if you could help, we need a hand with serving plates of food as the Doctors and Matron dish up the roast.

After a short break Candy met up with Shirley and began to help. The Matron handed out three types of plates that were for certain requests. "Wow there is a ton of variety here," Candy was surprised. "Candy, can you help me grab food from the kitchen as each of the trays are emptied and need replacing inside the bain-marie?" Tom asked anxiously.

"Sure, you can count on me."

"Excellent, thank you Candy you are a life saver. "Did you know the word bain-marie is a French term that directly translates to Mary's bath. I hope that is not the virgin Mary," Tom explained on their way to the main kitchen.

Shirley was having small talk between a few nurses. In agreeance she could do further education early to get qualified as an assistant in nursing. Find information and report to registered staff and in some cases the on-duty doctor. "Luckly, I come from a supportive, stable and smart family that will make this transition into nursing easy."

Then without warning Candy rushed through holding a tray calling out excitedly. "I got the lactose free beans; I got the lactose free beans."

The room became dead silent as over one hundred and fifty people stared at Candy. "I got the lactose free beans," Candy stated proudly. Shirley and Brett noticed Rosealina staring from the kitchen with a smug look on her face. The Matron asked curiously. "Lactose free beans, what are they?"

One nurse answered, "they are marked up ten dollars a pound. All the nurses and Shirley laughed with Candy. Though Candy thought they were laughing at her.

Candy walked with her head held high going into the staff room. Sitting at the table she lowered her head and began to cry. Tom Henderson walked in and sat across from her. "I have heard a few things today and let me reassure you are not at fault here. Rosealina is a nasty piece of work."

Candy continued to cry. "I do not understand why everyone is mean. But my sister is mean to me laughing at me with everyone else."

"Candy, they laughed because you made a joke even though it was unintentional. Most who reside here need a friend."

Tom began telling Candy a story about Christmas. "Let me tell you a Christmas story for the book you and Shirley are working on. One year at a family gathering it was the family game of secret Santa or anti secret Santa. Each person grabs a number out of a hat and one by one each person grabs a present from the table or takes one from someone who has a present and then they have a turn to claim one or steal one. Get my story so far?"

Candy nodded. "When Patrick was five, he got ticket number one. He grabbed the biggest box and I mean his face to choose the first present was a look I only saw once. Then a distant relative and then my sister Jill grabbed the present off him, and he had to choose another and another since you cannot repossess the present back."

Candy sobbed, "that is so awful. It sounds heart breaking and messy."

"Well, it got worse through two more relatives taking his present. So, on my turn I got the original present and told everyone it was for Patrick so for no one to touch it. Then when it was Uncle Denial's turn, I said get fucked being stern. This splits up the Henderson family and more importantly our family created our own traditions now on Ravenscroft Lane. Also, my father has never intended to celebrate Christmas he always blamed mom no matter how many Christmases she has not been with us."

"Patrick loves you unconditionally," Candy reassured lovingly.

"Yes well, it is hard to explain to a five-year-old what is happening in this Secret Santa game when assholes purposely take your present. The present then remained wrapped for Christmas morning. Then last night I was listening to you and your sister while you were giving him a therapy session."

Candy grimaced realising they certainly said a few inappropriate things.

"I did not realise the pressure we put on him about his birthday, so it is time for his Christmas miracle to come true. Rest assure I intend to help your Hell house each night because on Ravenscroft Lane we are not just neighbours, we are family. I feel your part of my family as a relative who will be sad for the day you move out of Ravenscroft Lane then a relative who is happy seeing you grow up and be happy."

Candy wiped her tears as her father came though crying. "That asshole Mr. Fredricks has just taken the Christmas spirit right out of me."

Tom frowned angrily towards Mark for his outburst.

"Then again, everyone is laughing at your lactose free beans joke." Candy stood as she hugged Mark tightly. "Thank you for helping everyone today. You and your sister are truly the best family any father could ask for."

Mark cried out still in stitches from the lactose free beans joke. "I better get out there since I am paid on the clock," Mark said as he left the room.

Tom Henderson stood up and continued explaining. "Sometimes in life we are mistaken and yet we find ourselves making mistakes to learn from for Christmases yet to come."

Candy asked one more question curiously. "After all that for Patrick and the Secret Santa family dramas you didn't tell me what was in that present for him Christmas morning."

Tom Henderson took a deep breath then exhaled shamefully. "It was a Roudolph the red nose reindeer sex doll."

As the day ended the Garrison and Henderson family began to agree completely more to simply enjoy the Christmas season not putting pressure Christmas day. Ms Patterson was a poet and not everyone knew it. Authoring a poem dedicated to Candy she made copies and gave them to all who reside at Gwenvale Nursing Home. This is that poem.

Lactose-free Beans

Candy's bringing something special today.
To the Christmas party for the elderly.
Steamed to perfection, with no added sheen.
Her lactose-free beans, oh what a sight
Simple, the most wholesome cuisine.

No added ingredients of any kind.
Just the beans and their natural Flavors.
Candy's dish could not be more refined.
A simple pleasure that most definitely savours.

The guests sneer at the sight of the beans.
But Candy remains steadfast in her belief.
Telling everyone, "Just give it a scene."
It is her resolve that brings everyone such relief.

As they eat, the guest's delight and surprise.
There is nothing more heavenly than these.
Candy's lactose-free beans were a hit, they realize.
Leaving everyone feeling happy and at ease.
So, the guests asked for Candy's recipe.
But she just smiled and kept it to herself.
Her secret, or her just her decree.

But as delicious as the beans may be,
There is a downside that we must see.
For oftentimes, after the feast,
Comes a bout of flatulence, unbridled, at least.

It is a common occurrence in elderly folks,
A common part of aging, as science evokes.
But that does not make it any less embarrassing,
For the elderly who cannot stop expelling.

So, while Candy's lactose-free beans are divine,
We must be prepared for the flatulence that will chime.
Some digestive aids can be on hand,
To help ease the discomfort of the elderly clan.

CHAPTER 8

HELL HOUSE

Two weeks until Christmas where nurses are preparing residents to see the lights throughout the neighbourhood. Candy, Shirley, and their mother Melissa are at Ravenscroft Lane where the scene is set. Meanwhile Mark is volunteering his time for the bus ride that may not be worth a dime, while the driver sings a tune that is out of line. As the night grew darker and the twinkle of Christmas lights beckoned, Mark found himself facing a daunting challenge - loading a bus full of elderly folks for a merry sightseeing adventure. With canes, walkers, and a few mischievous wheelchairs, the task seemed almost impossible. But Mark, determined as ever, donned his Santa hat, and embraced the holiday spirit.

First up was Mrs. Jefferson, a sprightly lady with a quick wit and a penchant for slow walks. She huffed and puffed, insisting she could tackle the bus steps without assistance. As she hesitantly climbed onboard, her dignity intact, Mark secretly celebrated his small victory. But just when he thought they might be on their merry way, chaos ensued. Mr. Thompson, a jolly gentleman with a passion for snacking, was determined not to leave his box of gingerbread cookies behind. Crumbs trailed behind him like Hansel and

Gretel's breadcrumbs, causing a slippery obstacle course for the others. It took the combined efforts of nursing staff to kick the trail off the bus.

One of the nurses offered Mr. Fredricks a wide brimmed Christmas hat that has elves' legs peeking out from the front. "Oh yes, I will take that hat Mr. Fredriks cheered enthusiastically. Being pushed in a wheelchair Mr. Fredricks sang out, "lovers in the air."

There was temporary parking for wheelie walkers as bums are sitting on seats. "Good news Mark Mr. Fredricks is coming is their room for another wheelchair?"

Mark sighed heavily. "One base here it can only fit wheelchairs on one side not both sides. This was a miscalculation from my part. We already have those who need a comfortable wheelchair to compromise and sit on seats. If he can do that then sure."

Mr. Fredricks heard what Mark explained. "No way. I want to be on this bus ride in a wheelchair and that is final."

One nurse raised her hand. There is the minibus, I can take him in it since there is room to strap in a wheelchair."

After an inconvenient compromise Mr Fredricks was on the minibus alone and ready to go. Little did the staff know one resident was dressed up wearing his tinsel hat forgotten by everyone since he has troubles speaking clearly.

Finally, the bus revved up, ready to tackle the streets ablaze with festive lights. Little did the residents of Gwenvale Nursing Home know, the mirth-filled journey had a joyous twist in store. The bus driver Harold possessed a Christmas spirit of toxic positivity that outweighed his sense of direction.

As they set off, turning down street after street in search of shimmering spectacles, Harold's navigation skills began to falter. He wheeled left when he should have turned right, and occasionally circled the same block for an encore where there were no lights to be seen. The passengers, a mix of amusement and frustration, held on tightly to their seatbelts, like bewildered reindeer on a rollercoaster sleigh ride.

With each wrong turn, the bus became a magnet for Christmas chaos. Enormous inflatable snowmen waved cheerfully at their misfortune, tangled strands of lights winked mockingly, and synchronized holiday music played on, oblivious to their joyride gone astray.

But amidst the laughter and sighs, the passengers found solace in their shared misadventure. They became a true band of merry misfits, exchanging stories of holidays past and present, and singing carols fitfully off-key. The bus became a mobile haven of friendship and merriment, despite its confused trajectory.

Eventually, after countless detours and comedic wrong turns, Harold managed to find the ultimate display of Christmas lights. The passengers, their cheeks rosy and hearts full of laughter, piled out of the bus onto the illuminated street. They marvelled at the shimmering wonderland before them, feeling like they had embarked on an accidental holiday adventure on none other than Ravenscroft Lane.

Ms Loretta Patterson spewed throughout the bus creating unexpected chaos as one of the nurses shouted scaring Harold the bus driver. "Oh my god she vomited everywhere. She has box wine in her handbag." In a moment of shock Harold temporarily lost control as the bus came to a complete stop.

As Mark watched the residents' gleeful faces, he could not help but feel that sometimes, the unplanned detours lead to the most memorable moments. Residents observed the lights on Ravenscroft Lane surrounded by lights and the shared understanding that the true magic of Christmas lies in the joy we create, regardless of the journey we take.

Meanwhile the minibus came to an abrupt halt. Mr. Fredricks noticed his house on Ravenscroft Lane has people coming and going. Leaving everyone behind he stormed over to see what was going on. Noticing his front patio was set up to look like Ebenezer Scrooges counting house. Children who lived on Ravenscroft Lane held out a tin asking for a gold coin donation. "Bah humbug," Mr. Fredricks walked inside ignoring the little girl dressed in green with pigtails as he walked into his home.

"Follow me everyone as we look at Jacob's warning," a scrawny looking kid said giving a tour for twelve. Mr. Fredricks noticed another kid organising another tour group saying they need twelve people at a time. Mr. Fredricks stood back watching the tour given from his bedroom. "What is that prick doing in my bed wearing my pyjamas? What is up with that ghost in chains?" It was like no one was listening to Mr. Fredricks enjoying the performance displayed.

"But Jacob you were always a good man of business."

"Mankind should have been my business. Oh, woe is me in these chains I built for myself in life," the ghost of Jacob wailed. "I made chains for myself in this life never leaving the counting house. Your chains are thicker and heavier unless you change your ways."

"But Jacob, what am I supposed to do?"

"You will be visited by three ghosts and the first one will come when the clock strikes one."

Ebenezer Scrooge looked at the audience and bowed. "I will head to the next room and see you all there." Scurrying past everyone into the next room the tour guide did a quick reflection of the scene they witnessed then progressed the next room to look at Scrooges past. Mr. Fredricks decided to follow keeping a low profile since it was his home, and he did not tell anyone from the Gwenvale Nursing Home bus ride where he went.

Watching performers move cardboard frames changing the setting from a classroom to outdoors where Scrooge lost the person he loved most to selfish pride and greed.

"You loved me once," Candy said playing the part of Belle while the elderly man of Ebenezer Scrooge was pretending to also be younger for the scene.

"Business continues to be poor. Investments have not returned as promised therefore we must delay the wedding another year."

Mr. Fredriks laughed, "kiss her before she leaves you." A little girl in green and blonde pigtails laughed standing next to Mr. Fredricks. "Your funny," she giggled being asked to be quiet for the performance. Mr. Fredricks winked.

"Why do you delight in torching me spirit?"

"These are the things of the past. They are what they are do not blame me."

Performers prepared for the next scene as the tour guide reflected on how the story missed the scene with Scrooges boss and how he met Belle. He did mention good points about the finances and yet as his boss said Christmas is a time for generosity.

"Thank you all for attending my Christmas themed Hell House my name is Candy and yes, I played the part of Belle and yes, my father named me Candy due to his O.C.C.O.D. Obsessive Compulsive Christmas Obsessive Disorder. While they are setting up the next room, I have gift bags donated by some shop for each night until a week before Christmas."

Mr. Fredriks notice the little girl in her green dress and pigtails getting excited. "You can have mine little girl he said cheerfully. Avoiding Candy, he stepped aside while the girl asked Candy if she could have Mr. Fredricks bag.

Peeking into the third bedroom he noticed Tom Henderson inside a large puppet playing the Ghost of Christmas Present. Waving to Tom Henderson who was distracted organising himself inside the oversized puppet.

"Screw you to for taking over my house," Mr. Fredricks growled under his breath. Making his way outside joining another group performing in a make-believe cemetery where another Ebenezer Scrooge performer was begging to the Melissa who was performing as The Ghost of Christmas Yet to Come.

"I beg you spirit to have mercy on my soul." The ghost of Christmas Yet to Come waved to Mr. Fredricks revealing her face under the hooded cloak to be Melissa Garrison. At the end of the performance Melissa began to explain everything to Mr. Fredricks. "Since your fall the neighbourhood has raised donations at the door and various sponsorship to pay for your medical bills while you are in the nursing home."

"I have heard lots of bullshit over the years, and this is the worst considering all neighbours harassing cause my accident. But now I walk better than I have in years and out of the wheelchair."

At that time, she pointed towards her husband Mark approaching. "Oh, here come the asshole who put me in the nursing home." Mark walked past Mr. Fredricks crying. Shocked by Marks ignorance Mr. Fredricks grinded his teeth wondering what he was going to say. "The bus came to a sudden stop where the minibus crashed behind. Paramedics have been trying but Mr. Fredricks is dead."

Stunned Mr. Fredricks turned to look down the street noticing the ambulances and police line keeping pedestrians out. "That is my body on a stretcher. Oh no my head, my head is a mess." Mr. Fredrick tried to touch his head feeling his hand pass through.

"It will be all right Mr. Fredricks. You know and I know you no longer belong here, so you need to find the light," Melissa cried realising that she was talking to his ghost. Mark shivered. His ghost is here? "Mr. Fredricks, I need to return to the bus, and you need to cross into the light."

"Wait, you can see me and the little girl in green with the pigtails was talking to me. You can help me return to my body or cross into the light?"

"Oh, piss fuck. Moving to Ravenscroft Lane was supposed to be stress free." Melissa sighed heavily.

For the days ahead Mr. Fredricks realised he was earth bound to his home and Ravenscroft Lane unable to leave the neighbourhood.

CHAPTER 9

DECK THE HALLS

Melissa had always believed in the magic of Christmas. The twinkling lights, the warm aroma of freshly baked cookies, and the joyous laughter of loved ones filled her heart with warmth.

However, this Christmas is miserable since the ghost of Mr. Fredricks was consistently engaging in conversation. Melissa's initial shock from the other night quickly turned to curiosity and empathy. She gazed at Mr. Fredericks with concern and compassion, his ghostly presence tugging at her heartstrings. She knew she had to help him find peace and the elusive Christmas spirit he sought.

"Alright, Mr. Fredricks I have a series of questions to ask to see if your death is even Christmas related or if there is something else keeping you earthbound." Mark passed through the living room realising that his wife was talking to the ghost of Mr. Fredricks. "Just putting up some decorations on the roof. Do you mind holding the ladder since this project is heavier than normal?"

Melissa sighed, "can't you see I have not slept properly for three days? I am helping Mr. Fredricks since he is earth bound to this Merry-pissed neighbourhood."

Mark realised from years of marriage that now he needs to give her space and deal with his own problems.

"I will figure something out. As for you Mr. Fredricks, I hope you learned something from pushing to get your own way. If you listened to reason, then perhaps there would not be a need for the minibus since you refused to participate without a wheelchair that you clearly did not need," Mark asserted himself looking around wondering where the ghost of Mr Fredricks was.

"Mark, nagging won't help," Melissa growled watching Mark leave quickly.

"Wheelchair?" Melissa stared glaring at the ghost of Mr Fredricks.

"Do not judge me. I had reasons to be in a wheelchair at that time."

Melissa cringed, "It's your business though now to build trust and to make this work I will no longer call you Mr. Fredricks."

"But that is my name, you need to respect your elders."

"It is easier to help you if you tell me your name. This way we are equals in this process otherwise if you continue being an asshole then you are a lost cause and not worth my time."

Mr. Fredricks exaggerated his emotions making a mockery of his unfortunate situation. "Oh no, since dying I cannot remember my name. Being a ghost has made me forget my name and my past."

Mellias stared for a moment, "I think my husband needs help on the roof I should go help him since he is not wasting my time."

"Kimberly and before you judge it is because of my father's heritage in south Korea where his surname was Kim. It is common like smith in English speaking countries. Then language barriers caused a miss communication."

Melissa laughed pressing her lips together. "Okay, Kimberly." Grunting louder as she laughed hysterically. "I will stick to Mr. Fredricks. Since we are doing this, I need to make a cuppa." Melissa did not realise that her husband Mark could be seen from the window with a rope tied to one leg hanging from the rooftop.

*   *   *

Walking along Ravenscroft Lane was none other than Tom and Sarah Henderson seeing Mark in his predicament. "Are you alright Mark?" Tom asked franticly pulling him upward while Sarah pulled out her Swiss Army knife cutting the rope. Mark was assisted by Tom falling safely. "Thank you, Tom and Sarah," Mark thanked them shaken fearfully.

"Geeze Mark. You should be more careful when putting up decorations." Tom looked to see fiberglass reindeer and a Seigh that could fit two people in. "Have you gone mad. I mean look at this Sleigh its running rings out of this year's decorations. How did you get it onto the roof?"

Mark stood proudly, "a simple Pullie system helped from the attic above. This will add more to the neighbourhood complementing Hell house across the street." Sarah smiled then her eyes widened seeing Melissa talking to no one since she could not see Mr. Fredricks. "Come with us Mark and I will show you what I have done. If you scratch my back for a few chores, then I can help you finish what you are doing on that rooftop."

Making way to the end of Ravenscroft Lane where one house looks down on all in the neighbourhood. Tom's home was by far the most desirable house from where he had plans for opening parts of his home to influence his chances to win the individual award for the best Christmas themed home in all Gwenvale "Let me show you the last stop on our tour to bask in the true beauty of community," Tom said sounding surer of himself.

Following a path to the right side of the home Tom had an elevator recently installed designed for wheelchair access to the rooftop patio lined with thick steel safety rails. "Step inside the elevator and Sarah will meet us up there soon," Tom insisted. Moving upward smoothly enjoying the elevator ride. "Now take a good look at Ravenscroft Lane from the best view in all Gwenvale," Tom held his arm out as Mark stood in all awe.

"I can see everything from here," Mark gasped in amazement. "I can see most of Gwenvale forest and town from this spot. There is the nursing home where I work oh and the school. It is picturesque." Sara stepped out from the attic door placing a tray onto a nearby table. "Care for some hot chocolate and nibbles?" Sarah offered. Mark gracefully accepted some hot chocolate adding marshmallows. Sarah noticed Michelle crossing the road looking as if she were frustrated talking to someone using hand gestures.

"How about you go back with Mark and help him and Melissa to finish what they have started since their sleigh will add more character to the neighbourhood?"

"Excellent idea my love. My services are available to you Mark just tell me what I can do to help."

Marks eyes widened, "do you really want to help? What about the competition are you striving for first place?"

Tom grinned, "you came to our home and got to know us better man. It is not about my ego any longer. This year we come together more than ever for Ravenscroft Lane and our community. Sure, I may still get first place for the best decorated house but now more than ever as we look around, we see Ravenscroft Lane and its families happier getting into the Christmas Spirit.

* * *

As Mark and Tom joined forces to improve Santa's sleigh Melissa was trying to help Mr. Fredricks.

"After going through a few of your belongings and listening to your rant I have determined three significant things to why you are earthbound."

"Tell it to me straight doctor," the Ghost of Mr Fredricks requested.

"You got divorced due to your wife spending too much for Christmas sending your two children into dire financial straits."

"It's hard since I was getting old fast and weak in the knees. Typical miner's wife knows how to spend into a new lifestyle as opposed to investing long-term avoiding aged care living," the ghost of Mr Fredricks responded smugly.

"Cut the attitude because the next point caught me by surprise."

The ghost of Mr Fredricks waved his hand gesturing for Melissa to continue. "You reference Christmas movies more than the nerds my husband hangs out with." Melissa asserted her hand forward and continued.

"You find Christmas joy in movies and books but struggle to see the funny side of fiction. Again, only reference movies and books if you're genuinely trying to heal from your past."

The ghost of Mr Fredricks nodded in agreeance. "You know the most tragic part of your story?

You have no idea on the whereabouts of your two sons despite having some memories in recent years."

"I blocked out over the years despite one son being Christmas obsessed and the other just enjoying the simple things despite random mishaps. Like my first attempt to create a gingerbread house using salt instead of sugar. For the family, all that mattered was spending quality time together." Without realising the ghost of Mr Fredricks shed a tear.

Melissa thought to herself to her surprise that she knows both sons who do not talk to each other. Part of the healing to is to get Mr Fredricks to have his own revelation in hope that his heart changes so he may cross into the light or be sucked into eternal darkness. In one way or another he has free will to decide from his heart what he wants.

CHAPTER 10

RAINDEER GAMES

Five days until Christmas the Garrison family enjoyed an early dinner since it was a Garrison family tradition for Mark and his friends to play their reindeer games throughout Gwenvale. Suddenly the phone rang. Candy let her father know the call was for him. Running like a child hooked on caffeine Mark answered the phone full of glee.

"Hey Brett, I have a perfect scavenger hunt planned and plenty of activities for this year's annual Garrison Family Reindeer Games Tradition.," Mark announced while Brett was holding the phone away from his ear. "Mark, its consistently short staffed in the nursing home so I will be starting earlier and following on with the night shift."

Mark sighed angrily, "not enough staff as always. Oh, all right then I guess we can make it work with just the three of us." Mark pouted.

Returning to the dinner table. "We are short this year and we need a fourth member to join us."

Melissa smirked sounding loving in her words, "Ask Tom to be your fourth. Afterall, he did set up the Sleigh for you to enjoy. Then he cleaned the guttering. Then he shovelled the driveway since even now the weather is forecasting more snowfall. He also worked at Hell house for seven nights straight for Candy and this neighbourhood. Oh, do not forget he fixed the dishwasher since you asked him."

"Alright I get the message. I will call him."

Michelle held up her phone. "I text him and he replied, 'on my way."

Knocking could be heard at the door. "Hey Mark, its Tom here. I got someone to cover me for Hell house tonight and boy I am keen for some Garrison Family shenanigans tonight."

Mark shouted that he was coming and thanked his wife sarcastically as he made his way to the garage. Candy and Shirley looked at their mother. Shirley began asking curiously, "so if reindeer games are a family tradition for four then why is the family tradition all about what dad wants?"

Mark started up his car with Tom in the passenger seat while the ghost of Mr. Fredricks sat in the back testing his chances to see if he could finally leave Ravenscroft Lane. Driving through to the end of Ravenscroft Lane waiting for a break in traffic.

"This is your chance. Get me past this damn boundary line," the ghost of Mr. Fredricks demanded. Then he stared at Tom unsure on who he was, yet he seemed more familiar than most in the neighbourhood. In a tight moment Mark turned off Ravenscroft Lane speeding up eager to see his friends. The ghost of Mr. Fredricks however, was hit by an unknown barrier that would not let him pass.

"Noooo," the ghost of Mr Fredricks shrieked.

Mark drove through the neighbourhood with Tom in the passenger seat as they picked up his two friends Craig and John. Tom held reservations introducing himself. "Since your new to this tradition Tom we have a few rules to cover. First, I dress as Santa since driving. Since you are passenger, you get to dress up as Roudolph guiding our way."

Craig sighed laughing, "oh, I wanted to be Roudolph this year since it was my idea to include ornament dropping after we deliver all the gifts."

Tom grimaced, "gifts?"

"We drive around to everywhere where Roudolph says delivering presents anomalously to random households. Craig and John will deliver and when opportunity presents itself all while getting snapshots of the ugliest Christmas sweaters."

"What are we waiting for? Like a boy scout dating a cougar, we must be prepared," Tom smirked.

Mark carefully adjusted his fluffy white beard as he gazed at his reflection in the rearview mirror. He took one last look at his red velvet Santa suit and grinned, feeling the Christmas spirit fill the air. Today, he was on a mission to bring joy to the lesser fortunate households in town, and he had enlisted his new friend Tom to accompany him on this merry adventure.

Tom dressed as Rudolph with a shiny red nose, sat in the passenger seat clutching a crumpled sheet of paper containing a list of addresses. He looked out the window, his eyes twinkling with anticipation, as Mark revved the engine and the car roared to life. It was an old red station wagon, but with the reindeer antlers and red nose sporting the hood, it seemed transformed into a magical vehicle.

Each time they approached a household on the list, Tom would quickly direct Mark to turn left or right with excitement in his voice. The car zigzagged through the neighbourhood, spreading holiday cheer one street at a time.

Craig and John's presence added an extra touch of whimsy to their endeavour as they trotted alongside the car, occasionally hopping onto the sidewalk to prance around and jingle bells to create an illusion of reindeer-powered transportation.

As the journey unfolded, they faced minor conflicts that tested their Christmas spirit. Cars honked impatiently at the unconventional Santa undertaking, and some passersby shook their heads in disbelief. Mark remained undeterred, keeping a cheerful smile on his face, for he knew the true magic of the season lay in spreading joy to others, no matter how unconventional the mode of transportation.

"Pull over to that house. It could do with some Christmas cheer," Tom directed. Mark pulled near a small, worn-down house where an older gentleman came running out and gestured at him angrily. John rushed to apologize, explaining they were there to deliver presents. The man's eyes softened, and he chuckled, realizing his mistake. He thanked John for his efforts and offered him an alcoholic bottle of apple cider. John bowed like an elegant princess accepting the perfect fuel to continue their journey.

Another pause of disbelief occurred as they pulled up to an apartment building, where sceptical tenants curiously peered through the windows. A single mother, overwhelmed by the holiday stress, emerged teary-eyed as she watched Craig and John dressed as reindeer companions bring gifts for her children. The disbelief faded from her face, replaced by a radiant, grateful smile that warmed Mark's heart.

Throughout their merry adventure, Mark and Tom shared laughter, stories, and challenges. They encountered houses that had moved, or addresses that did not exist, breaking into bewildered fits of giggles. Thanks to Tom's guidance, they always found their way, surprising the grateful recipients with unexpected presents and spreading joy wherever they went.

By the end of the day, their car had become a staple figure in the neighbourhood, their jingling bells and cheerful laughter echoing through the streets, announcing the arrival of Santa Claus and his faithful reindeer. As they shared a moment of quiet reflection in the cozy glow of the car's interior, Mark could not help but feel that the true magic of Christmas had revealed itself.

In those minor conflicts and random moments of disbelief, the strength of their collective determination and the power of kindness had shone through, proving that Christmas miracles could happen, even in the most unexpected ways.

"Tom, we will be honoured to have you join us next year. Our usual friend Brett puts work before leisure."

"Only if your friend cannot make it. I am sure he needs this social occasion more than I do," Tom suggested then he looked out the car window thinking about his younger brother Brett and what should, could or would have been this time of year.

After a long day of bringing joy to households, Mark, Tom, Craig, and John decided to make a quick detour before the day's end. They headed towards Craig's home, where a forty-year-old still lives with his mother. As they approached, the warm glow of Christmas lights illuminated the cozy house, welcoming them inside.

Entering the house, the sweet scent of freshly baked cookies and freshly brewed eggnog filled the air. Mrs. Johnson an older woman greeted them with a warm smile, her eyes twinkling with delight at the sight of Santa and the reindeer. "Come in, come in! I am so glad you all could stop by," she exclaimed, ushering them into the kitchen where a lovely spread awaited them.

Mrs. Johnson, a gentle and kind soul, had been busy baking all day. On the kitchen table sat intricately decorated cookies, shaped like Christmas trees, snowflakes, and gingerbread men. The sight was dazzling, like a miniature winter wonderland. Beside them sat glasses of creamy eggnog, sprinkled with a hint of nutmeg.

"Gather around and tell me what you think?"

Tom dipped his gingerbread cookie into the eggnog and took a big bite. "These are nice Miss Johnson, but I have had better. My mum makes the best cookies but please do not tell my wife."

"With an attitude like that I would put coal in your stocking. You should help your wife in the kitchen or at least appreciate her qualities not to compare her to your mommy," Craig huffed.

"I am not the one living with mommy," Tom insulted. "Well, at least Christmas has brought us all together to try different recipes. Just be glad you are not trying Michelles cookies for some reason they taste salty," Mark began wondering.

Miss Johnson laughed drawing attention to herself deescalating any unnecessary conflict. "If it is any consolation, I made my husband's coffee too strong so he would take us out for dinner occasionally. Until he got used to it that is."

As everyone gathered around the festive table, they chatted and laughed, their spirits lifted by the warmth of the house and the love-filled atmosphere. Mrs. Johnson told them with stories of Craig's mischievous childhood and shared her delight in their mission to bring holiday joy to others.

Filled with Christmas cheer, Mark and the group decided to enlist Mrs. Johnson's homemade delights for their next plan. They knew the business district could use some extra holiday spirit, so they decided to embark on a special Christmas ornament drop. They would attach ornaments, along with small bags of cookies, to random lampposts and park benches for passersby to find and enjoy.

With Mrs. Johnson's eggnog and cookies packed into a large wicker basket, the group bid farewell and headed back to the car. Mark, once again in his Santa Claus attire, spread the seat full of ornaments while Tom and John fastened the bags of cookies to each one. Tom climbed back into the car and took his place as a reindeer in the passenger seat.

As they reached the business district, Mark slowed the car down as Craig directed him to the perfect lamppost for the first ornament drop. With swift precision, John, and Craig attached a beautifully adorned ornament, each with a bag of cookies, to the lamppost. They stood back, admiring their handiwork and imagining the surprise and delight of the unsuspecting passerby who would stumble upon their festive treasures.

One by one, they continued their ornament drop, pausing occasionally to revel in the enchantment of their spontaneous act of kindness. Strangers passing by smiled and even joined in, helping with the endeavour. The business district transformed into a magical place, with ornaments twinkling in the lamplight and the aroma of freshly baked cookies permeating the air.

As they neared the end of their mission, the group huddled together, hugging one another, filled with gratitude and the knowledge that they had made a difference in the lives of others.

Little did they know, this magical day was just the beginning, as the ripple effect of their actions would spread joy everywhere, reminding everyone that the true spirit of Christmas lies in the joy found through giving and the bonds we create when we come together to make Gwenvalle a little brighter.

Mark parked the car desperately looking for his list of reindeer games. "Damn I cannot find the list. I had other games planned for tonight and now our night is ruined."

"Hey Craig, maybe we need to set him up with another citrus flavoured snow cone," John stated grinning.

"No thanks! It has a strange after taste."

"I am keen for another one gentleman," Tom requested not knowing how they made the snow cone.

"Thats right! Let us check out the competition for the best themed street in the neighbourhood.

As Mark, Tom, Craig, and John continued their journey through the neighbourhood, they noticed an array of vibrant Christmas lights illuminating the streets. The holiday spirit was in full swing, and one street caught their attention. The entire block was engaged in a friendly competition to create the most enchanting Christmas display.

Driven by curiosity, they decided to explore further and entered the street adorned with twinkling lights and festive decorations. As they marvelled at the creativity on display, they noticed that three houses, coincidentally next to each other, were each devoted to a specific Christmas theme.

The first house proudly displayed a Star Wars Holiday Special theme. The front yard was transformed into a galaxy far, far away, adorned with lightsabre-wielding jedi wearing Santa hats. A life-sized Chewbacca stood next to a colourful Christmas tree, and a little person in a Yoda costume greeted visitors with holiday-themed wisdom. Mark and his companions could not help but chuckle.

"Mark, I dare you to drive by as I shout some wisdom to Yoda," Tom laughed leaning out the window.

"Darth Jar-Jar Binks is the powerfullest force user." Gasping from all around from Jedi who passed the word on throughout the street.

"Wow what a rush," Tom banged his fist into his chest like a collage football jock. "Look at my hand it is all shaky. John leaned forward pretending to be his favourite Star Wars character, "Messa and Wesa are ready back here. Are Yousa ready to see the Baptist display in the dinky little cul-de-sac?"

"Sure," Mark confirmed driving to the cul-de-sac of five homes.

As they reached the cul-de-sac, they were greeted by a serene nativity scene radiating peace and tranquillity. Each figure, from Mary and Joseph to the baby Jesus, was beautifully illuminated, casting a soft glow across the entire cul-de-sac. Neighbors had come together to create a unified display, with each house contributing a different element of the nativity scene. Hearts filled with reverence as onlookers admired the thoughtful tableau commemorating the birth of Jesus.

"Meh it's a bit to basic and it's like they are copying the Baptists," everyone cheered simultaneously feeling like this year they will win on Ravenscroft Lane.

Moving along to Catilyn Street where everyone was amazed by the captivating Hell house themed from the classic book How the Grinch Stole Christmas. Residents and Baptists were dressed as if they belonged in Whoville. It was like driving through a movie set. "Look at that. A few have eggnog hats filled with actual eggnog like in the movie," Tom took a photo while reassuring Mark that they will outshine Catilyn Street.

Meticulously crafted Grinch statues lined in one yard, with the mischievous character depicted wearing Santa's hat and one Grinch sitting in a sleigh laden with gifts. Passersby eagerly posed for photos with the Grinch, capturing memorable moments of holiday cheer alongside the classic Christmas curmudgeon.

"I know we have more games ahead of us, but I think for tonight we need to compare and beat Catilyn Street at their own game," Mark explained.

Tom sighed heavily, "I have met my match here tonight and my winning streak is over yet again. There is no way we can compete with a Grinch who gives gifts and instant professional photos to anyone passing by." Little did they realise Craig and John were getting their photo taken with the man dressed as the Grinch.

"My house."

"What?" Tom said shocked.

"I have the sleigh on the roof top. From there we do an ornament drop with the parachutes like we did earlier but from the rooftop it is more a Christmasy kind of Christmas."

Craig and John got back into the car with their photos, presents, candy canes and bottles of eggnog. "Alright guys we need your help this year more than ever before."

Quickly driving back to Craig's home, the four asked Craig's mother for more baked goods to do another ornament drop. With in an hour, they created quite an assembly line creating three hundred ornaments. "Alright let us go," Mark ordered.

"Not so fast."

Craigs mother smiled. "I have spent twelve hours in the kitchen and helped every year. I am coming with you."

"Great, the more the marrier," Mark confirmed realising the pressures he placed on her.

Everyone got into the car with Craigs mother sitting in the front seat and Tom squeezed between John and Craig. Reaching Marks house, the four men made their way onto the roof ready for the ornament drop.

Craig's mother stood next to Melissa as Shirley prepared her video camera to record their performance. Tom noticed some spare rope inside the attic. "Tie this to yourselves Craig and John and play pretend to be reindeer with me pulling the sleigh." All set Mark raised his voice in hopes for the neighbours and spectators to see.

"It Twas the night before Christmas when Santa came," Mark said barely drawing any attention.

"Louder dad," Shirley shouted drawing attention from those touring Hell House. Mark pulled out an emergency box under his seat shooting a flare from a flare gun the attention was on him from everyone on Ravenscroft Lane. Raising his voice louder.

"It Twas the night before Christmas when Santa came bearing gifts, yet it seemed to be snowing like never before." Mark threw a couple of handfuls of ornaments. Tom got into the spirt as Roudolph prancing forward not realising that a bolt snapped connecting the Seigh to the roof. Mark paused then continued as more gathered to see what he was doing.

"Here you go down there but remember kids, I know when you are sleeping, and I know when you're awake."

Mark threw heaps more ornaments as their parachutes opened safely falling to the neighbouring children. Tom shouted, "I will lead your way, Santa."

In a hard pull forward the sleigh came off the railings. Sliding forward Mark called out warning Craig and John to jumped aside realising that they were tied to the sleigh. Suddenly the sleigh picked up speed hitting Tom's backside knocking him inside the sleigh as well. In a sudden flash the ghost of Mr. Fredricks called to Melissa, "That is Tom. He is one of my two sons. Shit! He is in danger."

Falling from the two-story roof they hit the footpath beneath hard. Since Ravenscroft Lane is on a hill the sleigh picked up more speed with John and Craig running alongside holding onto the sleigh.

Passing by a police car that came to see where the flare was shot from. Sliding uncontrollably past other cars that came to witness the festive lights the sleigh took a sharp turn for the worst. Descending through another road. Tom Pulled John in while Mark pulled Craig into the sleigh.

"Mark, if I die will you tell my wife I love her."

"What the hell are you on about?"

Mark stated trying to remain confident not knowing that Tom has untied the rope from himself. Jumping from the sleigh acting as an anchor pressing his feet into the snow and lowering his buttocks. "Is it slowing down?"

"Whatever are you doing it is working?" Sirens are heard quickly closing into their location. As the sleigh slowed down a police car met them as it came to a halt.

CHAPTER 11

CRAZY NIGHT SHIFT

The next morning Mark and Tom found themselves in court ordered to cease all Christmas activities on Ravenscroft Lane pending an investigation for placing people in the community at risk.

"I told you we needed a Lawyer. Maxwell Turner is who we needed to hire," Tom blamed Mark.

"I am done. I should take one from Mr Fredricks book and be the Asshole who did not want to celebrate Christmas. At least this way Our family could just enjoy it in peace."

Leaving separate ways with their wives both men returned to their homes. Marks home was covered in police lines keeping neighbours away. "There is more police tape around our home than Christmas decorations." Mark drove his car through stretching the tape into his carport. Closing the garage door, the tape stretched further. "Mark I cannot open my door the tape is pressed against the door. Angrily Mark pressed and pressed his door until the tape snapped causing a jerking motion pressing against himself.

"I got it now," Melissa explained avoiding any eye contact with Mark since he was in an unpleasant mood.

"Look at the asshole who lives at Thirty Ravenscroft Lane." Mark moaned to his wife. The ghost of Mr. Fredricks tried to communicate with Mark but to no avail. "I need to go to bed and get sleep before night shift. My Christmas spirit has been sucked right out this year," Mark refused to show any emotion besides anger.

The ghost of Mr. Fredricks waved to Melissa, "Tom is my son. He was the one who was obsessed with Christmas since his mother mostly raised him. I am beginning to remember."

"Then go to your son and leave my family alone. Can't you see we have our own problems to deal with?"

The ghost of Mr. Fredricks grimaced. "What do you mean by that? Are you not going to help me?"

"I never asked to see ghosts or to help them. I tried to help you, but you are a cynical old fart who can remain earthbound for all I care. Or here is a point. What is the difference between a Christmas turkey and Mr, Fredricks? The turkey has less shoved up its arse."

Mr. Fredricks for the first time in years felt remorse for how he acted throughout the whole Christmas Season. Leaving the Garrison family, he floated to see his son Tom crying while looking at his picture in a trophy cabinet.

"Christmas was fine until Mark moved in. Why did my brother have to give up on Christmas and never talk to me about it?'

Sarah sighed dramatically, "when will you wake up to the fact that not everyone has to celebrate Christmas? Have you ever wondered why it was so bad for your father who clearly never healed from how the true meaning of Christmas gets lost?"

Tom whimpered, "I am now the asshole who did not want to celebrate Christmas. Each year I drag you and Patrick down not to forget that we have a niece I have no relationship with all because I have not made up with my brother."

Sarah remained silent and listened to her husband seeing if he works things out. "Oh, if my father could hear me now. I am sorry for pushing you away all these years. I should have tried to have a relationship that was not Christmas as the focus."

The ghost of Mr. Fredricks shed tears. "If only you could hear me and understand Christmas sent us into financial ruin because your mother tried endlessly to recreate everything perfectly to the point, she blew more money than all donations to any local charity drive. I could not earn enough money on her terms. I just broke down that one Christmas when she blew twenty grand and then by easter we had an eviction notice for not paying rent. She belonged on an episode of Hoarders but then I stayed angry never trying to forgive her even though I know that the reason I am still be earth bound."

* * *

Mark woke up after struggling to sleep realising it Twas the night before the night before Christmas. Heading to do the night shift at Gwenvale Nursing

Home as a registered nurse placed him and Joanne in charge of six Assistants in Nursing. Two staff to a unit registered staff occupied the North and South unit while the other occupied the East and West unit.

Rosalina prepared food platers in the North unit dining room for staff to enjoy together. "Mark, with your permission once rounds are done, we can all take turns eating and enjoying in the Christmas treats that I have provided."

"Sounds good, I will go back to the south unit and send Brett to enjoy because I am feeling exhausted tonight."

Mark caught up with Brett and explained his predicament since now Christmas is cancelled on Ravenscroft Lane.

"Hey Brett, Rosealina has put out loads of platters for all the night staff since it is her last shift until after New Year's Day. I am not feeling the Christmas spirit tonight, so I just want to relax, eat a few snacks, and stay out of trouble tonight," Mark explained.

"You remember how I missed your reindeer games last night to come into work for overtime?"

"Yes." Mark replied confused.

"Well, Rosealina talked to me like a piece of shit making me out to be incompetent amongst other staff. She was mean to your daughter Candy setting her up for failure at the residents Christmas party. I have struggled to celebrate Christmas since my divorce Christmas day just like my father. So, for the last shed of Christmas joy left for my new wife of three years, I would like to enjoy a Christmas movie between answering buzzes and make going into Christmas eve a good day to remember."

Mark was gobsmacked unable to understand how Brett must be feeling especially only recently reconnecting with his daughter. Such a lively child visiting Hell house dressed in green and pretty blonde pigtails.

"I will go and let her know that you're not join in for Christmas snacks. Then in time I will come join you for a Christmas movie between doing rounds. Perhaps a movie will spark a shred of Christmas joy into my heart."

Heading to the North unit Rosealina grimaced seeing Mark instead of Brett. "Where is Brett?" Rosealina demanded an explanation.

"He said he doesn't want to join us tonight for nibblies. So, the rest of us can enjoy."

"Well, I'll go see to him now," Rosealina stormed through. Mark looked around noticing that staff had a plan taking turns to enjoy the food.

Rosealina peered from around the slattered wall noticing Brett watching the Muppets Christmas Carol while doing his paperwork. "Food is provided for all to enjoy."

Brett shook, "I am all fine thank you."

"Come on Brett, I do this each shift when I work on special holidays, no one is excluded when I put food on."

Brett remained steadfast, "I really don't feel like it I just want to enjoy the movie and get my work done."

"Stop being a party pooper. Tell me why you do not want to come," Rosealina demanded an answer. "I just want to be left alone tonight." Brett remained calm.

"Thats, not good enough. Christmas is for everyone."

Brett fired back, "Rosealina, you're a bitch."

Rosealina gasped as if she did not know she was a crazy bitch.

"What do you mean by that. It does not matter who is on the food is for everyone," Rosealina explained.

"The way you talked to me last night in front of staff, resident and their families is more reason for me not to give a crap."

"Swearing is not acceptable in the workplace. Now come on and join in."

"You're a crazy bitch and it is about time someone told you. Year after year you are mean to everyone and act like your perfect," now I just want to watch the movie in peace.

Rosealina would not let it go. "You just cannot handle that I am blunt. Brett pointed toward Rosealina then the corridor behind the slattered wall. "You miss the point. Fuck off!"

Rosealina stormed back to the north unit as the other staff clenched up enjoying the treats noticing Rosealina's attitude is aggressive. "Tell that ungrateful Humbug that he can remain alone."

Mark pretended to answer the portable work phone. "Alright I will be down in a jiffy." Then the phone rang for real as the staff knew he was pretending to find an excuse to leave. "Hello, Gwenvale Nursing Home Mark speaking."

"Hey Mark, it is your loving wife, Melissa. Mr Fredricks thinks there was a letter for you from him that may help him to cross over. So be a darling and read it."

"Okay, I'll be there in a jiffy," Mark said hanging up the phone making his way into the staff room grabbing the letter. Storming past the party he told everyone to continue without him for now as he headed back to the north unit.

The staff felt awkward around Rosealina who was still fuming.

"I'll join you soon Brett I just have a few things to check off," Mark said to Brett passing by then into the nurses' station checking off his checklist and then peacefully reading the note from Mr Fredricks.

Dear Mark

Since I am stuck in the nursing home, I am faced with a Christmas Dilemma. You must be sworn to secrecy since I am the Santa who delivers at Midnight before Christmas morning on Ravenscroft Lane. All Thirty houses need to share in the true spirit of Christmas as Santa makes his special delivery through the front door as all residents know to make passage for Santa.

I have written a list and checked it twice. A list of presents for everyone in all households including my own so gifts will not be forgotten and no one is missing out this Christmas. I have taken the liberty to circle and number each item.

Please I beg of you to keep the identity of Santa silent because it is the excitement that everyone enjoys. This year will you please be the Santa that Ravencroft Lane needs, and the Santa that Ravenscroft Lane deserves.

Kind Regards
Mr Fredricks

Mark began to sweat repulsively looking at item after item in the catalogue. Noticing twelve of the newest PlayStations quickly showed his list cost was multiplying. Since Mr Fredricks is dead, he would have to organise the funds himself to save Christmas on Ravenscroft Lane. Knowing it was after midnight since Melissa called Mark thought I better call her back before she falls asleep.

After a few rings Melissa answers the phone. "Who is dead. Someone better be dead."

"Sweetheart I reads the letter and I think I know how to help Mr Fredricks."

"Yep. What do you think it will take so I can get some sleep?"

Mark replied excitedly, "Mr Fredricks is the mysterious Santa on Ravenscroft Lane and if we don't fore fill this list he may not cross over."

"Wow that sounds like I need some sleep to go Christmas shopping on Christmas Eve," Mellisa mocked sarcastically.

"You get some sleep and I'll give you the list and credit cards while I sleep the day away ready to deliver the presents that night."

"Oh, bollocks, bugger, wanker, ninny McPhee piss it," Melissa held back a few more profanities. "You are going to stay awake and help me and the girls to do the shopping because if there is one thing, I will make clear about Christmas Eve shopping."

"Please tell me sweetheart," Mark asked curiously. "It's that I need sleep."

Melissa hung up the phone. "I think that went well," Mark said aloud to himself. Joining Brett in the lounge area he noticed Brett crying into a few tissues. "Is everything alright Brett?"

Brett nodded. "I have checked all rooms frequently and so far, an uneventful night shift."

Brett seemed remorseful from his incident earlier with Roselina he paused before asking Brett again. "What is the matter, Brett? Is there something wrong. Brett cried harder, "Tiny Tim died." Mark held his laughter back. "I won't spoil the ending for you though it's always tradition to watch this movie every year." Mark stopped talking realising family traditions are all about what he wants Christmas to be. His wife and two daughters watch the same repetitive movies for his sake not their own.

"It is because my children watch them to spend time with me. Also, you join in on reindeer games besides your divorce when Christmas was painful yet how do you heal Brett?"

Pausing the movie Brett faced Mark. "Alright, take a seat and I will tell you. One relationship went too fast and before I knew it, I was engaged Christmas day because I impregnated a single mum. Who I trusted with my credit cards and her idea of a perfect Christmas," Brett shrugged.

"I check my bank balances and find out it was nearly twenty grand just like what happened to my father as the reason to divorce my mother. Then for the first time I tried to return gifts to not have an empty bank account."

Brett grimaced for a moment, "I have to ask, is Mr Fredricks your father?"

"That he is. Though for years even with a daughter of my own and custody issues I have learned something valuable. Enjoy the season not just the day. My daughter enjoys the season and Christmas day she faces her mother's Christmas chaos. In time she can make her own mind up to enjoy the season or be caught in yet another crisis."

Mark began to realise that he had seen things wrong. "Brett, what is the reason that got you to heal from so much?"

"Spending Christmases with my wife and her grown up children and now grandchildren I have learned to block out the nonsense and focus on what is important. Without the pressures we enjoy life and argue less and less as we grow as people. Oh, also forget what I said to Roselina I am still in control of my emotions to enjoy Christmas with my family."

Mark shrugged, "I am sure she likes the self-portrait I had painted for her."

Brett chuckled while Mark had an idea to help Mr Fredricks.

"Before work tomorrow night how about you and your family come have dinner with us and have an open mind to what we have prepared. Think of it as a Henderson and Garrison dinner, games and sharing our Christmas jokes that come in cheap Christmas crackers."

CHAPTER 12

SHOPPING VIOLENCE

Christmas eve is the time for Christmas shopping amongst the masses of asses leaving their shopping to the last minute. Candy and Shirley shared zeal for holiday shopping with a meticulously planned a shopping extravaganza. Both had composed extensive lists of presents they aimed to buy for their father for filling the unexpected list shopping for seventy items between thirty houses.

However, they decided to add an unexpected twist this year by enlisting the help of the neighbouring teenagers, hoping to delegate tasks and complete their shopping more efficiently. Candy outlined the mission, handing three young teenagers a specific list of items and stores they needed to visit.

As the group marched out of the house, they were met with the hustle and bustle of the holiday shoppers. The streets were teeming with people, all decided to find perfect gifts. The first excitement and energy quickly escalated into chaos, as the teenagers scattered in different directions, each pursuing their assigned tasks.

"Alright Patrick, I need you to get this list of board games. Twenty-six to be exact."

Shirley anxiously watched Patrick disappear into a throng of shoppers going separate ways to obtain presents more suited for girls her age. Candy decided to accompany Robbie and Keith through a mega toy store to buy the latest action figures for the children on Ravenscroft Lane. Upon entering the store, the trio was met with long lines and cranky fellow shoppers.

"Where are the trollies?" Candy asked the boys seeing the trolly bay was empty.

"Carry basket will have to do," Keith said. Candy grabbed three baskets as they ventured through looking for the action figures. Robbie checked off three of seven items though noticed one figure line was completely sold out. "We can go elsewhere for it once we check here for all toys. Robbie had his eyes set on a kids ride on Jeep since it was also on the list. "I remember that hyperactive kid Lenny was after one of these."

Candy faced troubles with Rosalina trying to grab items out of her basket. Pushing and shoving Candy was found not to lose the other items on their list. "Let go crazy bitch," Candy slapped Rosalina then Rosealina slapped her back across her breast.

"Ouch," Candy shirked. Keith asked to hold her basket combining their items together checking off six of the seven action figures. While Candy and Rosealina were having it out Robbie is informed by a staff member that he needs a trolly to take the heavy item out of the shop, but he was determined to hold onto it until help arrives knowing that the kids ride on Jeep will sell faster than if he drove it out himself. Which the thought gave him an idea.

Rosealina grabbed Candy by the wrist and thigh determined not to let go until she handed over what she had. "It's just a couple of toys that we grabbed first."

Few shoppers gathered to seeing shopping chaos. "Leave Candy alone a few shoppers shouted asking that staff intervein. "Ho-Ho Haymaker," Rosalina announced for all to hear as she lined up the biggest slap that seemed to slow down for one epic attack.

"Get in," Robbie shouted to Candy who was driving the kids ride on Jeep that was clearly designed for a preschooler. Turning around Candy avoided the slap that connected to the store manager who was trying to stop Robbie for what he was doing.

Keith placed the basket into the kids ride on Jeep using a skipping rope to tie it down. Candy was told to leave safely and lovingly by the store manager. Gaining her breath, she was proud to see that they checked off everything from the toy shop except for one action figurine. "Still a few items to go but thanks to you two boys Christmas is saved on Ravenscroft Lane."

As they stood in line, patiently waiting, Keith spotted the last remaining action figure misplaced on one of the store shelves. Unable to hold his excitement, he snatched it before anyone else could get to it, unknowingly angering another customer who had been eyeing the same item.

The shopper, an impatient man confronted Keith shoving his shoulder, leading to an intense argument between the two. Candy, seeing the escalating conflict, swiftly intervened. "What is the capital of Thailand? She held her arm back then like a whip, she flicked the man in the dick shouting, "Bangkok."

Keith ran hiding the toy inside the kids ride on Jeep that Robbie was riding through the checkout.

*   *   *

Meanwhile, Patrick who had been tasked with picking out a choice of board games including three lots of classic Monopoly, found himself surrounded by shelves that were left messy. Feeling overwhelmed by the shopping list he thought to himself it is for Candy. What would I do for Candy?

While he was daydreaming about Candy blowing him a kiss, an older woman approached. "What board games do you like?"

Patrick remembered seeing her sunbaking from his patio since he used a telescope getting a better look of the gorgeous red-haired neighbour on Ravenscroft Lane. "Hello, I am Kerissa who lives five houses down from you."

"Oh, that's right," Patrick stuttered pretending that he did not know her so well.

"Do you need a hand to find anything?"

Patrick handed his list. "That is a lot of games and the same versions. "Why are you getting all this?" Kerissa asked curiously.

"I did not say this, but it is an emergency. It has been revealed that Mr. Fredricks has delivered the presents each year as Ravenscroft Lane's Santa. Now there is someone else taking over for Ravenscroft Lane and if this list is not fulfilled then many will not have as much of a Merry Christmas."

Kerissa's eyes widened.

"I so happens that I am an experienced board game enthusiast not to forget that Christmas cannot be cancelled on Ravenscroft Lane. Give me your list and I will retrieve the items and stay close to me it is a jungle in here," Kerissa explained.

Patrick thanked Kerissa for her help though he did not know how he was going to meet up with Shirley to pay for all this.

* * *

At the same time and same shopping centre Mark stumbled through the ladies clothing section with his wife Melissa pushing their trolley. He had just finished another gruelling night shift at Gwenvalle Nursing Home. His wife, Melissa knew how much Mark valued their new neighbours and could not bear the thought of disappointing them despite disappointing her every Christmas by lack of romance. Melissa carried a secret hope in her heart that her husband will find whatever meaning behind Christmas that he is yet to discover.

"Mark, dear," Melissa spoke gently, approaching her exhausted husband, "I know you're tired, but I need you to help me, help you with this list. Remember, the ghost of Mr. Fredericks is still lingering in our home binge watching Christmas movies in hope since he is still unable to cross over until we fulfil our commitment."

Mark sighed, rubbing his temples with weary hands. "I know, Melissa. It is just... I barely have the energy to keep my eyes open, let alone go out and brave the chaos of women's clothes shopping."

With a half-hearted smile, Mark agreed, "Alright, Melissa, let us do this. We have come so far, and I cannot bear to let our neighbours down. Just maybe, buying these presents will bridge the gap between our world and Mr. Fredericks' final rest."

Melissa guided Mark through women's lingerie her eyes scanning each aisle for inspiration. They needed to find thoughtful items from the list that would bring joy to their neighbours. As they explored the maze of clothing racks Melissa could see shameful guilt written on Marks face. "I am helping you otherwise we could get Candy and Shirley to model for you."

Mark nodded vigorously. "I am awake sweetheart."

Melissa grabbed several sets of lovely Christmas themed dresses realising that their neighbour Sarah was doing the same. Both women were in a lock realising that neither were going to let go of a fashionable silky dress.

"Melissa darling, I only need one size five dress," Sarah glared back at Melissa. "I need these dresses and to check off our list. Both women refused to let go continuing their squabble. In a moment of concern Mark pretended to faint since he was overtired after all. Sarah let go and went to Marks aid. Mark noticed his wife's unwavering focus and determination leaving the clothes department. "Sorry about that Sarah. My wife is under the pressure this holiday season."

"What did you say?"

"I pretend to faint and its code for her to run while you came to my aid."

Sarah's eyes widened. "No not that. You said happy holidays."

"Happy holidays. It is what we say not to offend anyone with different beliefs," Mark said.

Sarah spoke louder, "its Merry Christmas. Christmas is the reason our husbands send us shopping while they grab another alcoholic eggnog and enjoy Christmas."

Sitting up Mark apologised to Sarah about the clothes. Then he asked Sarah for help as she helped him search diligently, for clothes on the list and where abouts of his wife. After a few minutes of shopping and Sarah part ways Melissa watched Mark's tired frame slump onto a couch outside the dressing rooms.

"Mark, love," Melissa said softly, approaching her exhausted husband, "I know you're tired, but we got most things."

Candy sends a text message to Mark and Melissa.

I have what you asked for on this list. We saw you and mom in the women's section, so we thought it was best to wait outside with our trollies.

"Candy and Shirley are ready," Mark praised excitedly.

"Alright. Follow me to the checkout."

Melissa navigated the tumultuous sea of people, her eyes scanning every overcrowded aisle. Suddenly, a commotion erupted behind them, followed by loud voices and hurried footsteps.

Panic surged through his veins as he grabbed Melissa's hand and pulled her towards the exit. They sprinted through the crowd, weaving between frantic shoppers and dodging obstacles along the way. Mark's heart pounded in his chest as he desperately searched for a safe place to hide. He could not bear the thought of his family getting caught up in whatever dangerous situation was unfolding.

As he rounded a corner, he caught sight of Candy and Shirley huddled near the store entrance. Reaching the checkout loading up their items a crazy looking man approached excitedly. "Oh yes," he cheered clapping his hands together. Picking up the three different nerf guns he kissed them. "How much do you want for them?"

"Look they are not for sale," Mark told the man sounding exhausted.

"I will over five time the sticker price," the crazy man offered.

Melissa knew anyone in their right mind would not be that crazy. Grabbing the toys back she growled, "back away from the toys or I'll show a beast worse than Krampus."

Letting go of the presents the man backed away holding his hands out. After going through the checkout Melissa held her daughters close, a mix of fear and relief etched on her face. "We're all right Mom and Dad. A little shaken, though I see more crazy male shoppers than female shoppers. Thank goodness we found each other."

Melissa cringed noticing their family have a total of three trollies and a kids ride on Jeep tied up with three shopping baskets. "Seeing all this makes me wonder just how much money we have spent for Christmas. Ostrich affect is where we burry our heads in the snow and look at our bank account after Christmas," Mark explained.

"If Mr Fredricks crosses over tonight then I just do not care," Melissa said.

Mark exhaled deeply, grateful that his family was safe. Once returned home Melissa started the next phase of the Christmas plan. "Right, Mark you need to sleep so you have energy for tonight and before you return to work," Mellissa asserted.

"Candy and Shirley, you will watch Christmas movies and have engaging conversation with the ghost of Mr Fredricks regardless that you cannot see him. Just pretend he is there while you wrap up all the presents and remember all tags are written from Santa."

Mark hugged his wife thanking her for all her efforts. "What are you going to do while I have a sleep?"

"I am having a beer nogg before I talk to the neighbours?"

Mark grimaced, "you do not like egg nogg. Then what is a beer nogg?" Mark asked confused.

"It's where I tip egg nogg down the sink, then grab myself a beer."

"Mom that makes no sense," Candy stated confused.

The ghost of Mr Fredricks laughed at Melissa's joke. "As you Mr. Fredricks I will ask trivia questions about the next lot of movies, so you better get watching before tonight. You need a meaningful change of perspective, or you will not cross over into the light." Little did anyone realise that Candy glanced at the ghost of Mr Fredricks pretending that she cannot see him.

CHAPTER 13

THE ASSHOLE WHO GOT THE LAST LAUGH

That night Mark woke up to his alarm clock preparing himself since Brett was coming home for dinner with his wife and daughter. Candy and Shirley had six sacks loaded with presents that are to be distributed between thirty homes. They placed the six sacks at the back door ready for their father to do a late-night delivery. Melissa was busy in the kitchen for hours preparing a feast spread over two tables providing for ten people.

The wind howled outside, rattling the windows as Mark slowly stirred from his sleep. He opened his eyes to darkness, the room faintly illuminated by the soft glow of Christmas lights that adorned the house. He blinked away the remnants of slumber, his mind struggling to register the time.

As he sat up, his senses were engulfed in the scent of roasted turkey and freshly baked pies. Confusion washed over him before he remembered Melissa's plans for a Christmas Eve dinner party. He swung his legs over the side of the bed and slipped on his ridiculous jingle bell slippers, eager to join in the preparations.

Quietly, Mark snuck down the stairs trying to keep his jingle bell slippers from making a sound, careful not to disturb his wife's work in the kitchen. The aroma of warm spices and bubbling casseroles grew stronger as he descended, filling his senses with anticipation for the night to come. The faint sound of merry chatter reached his ears, saying Brett and his family had already arrived.

"Wow honey, what an amazing set up," Mark complimented looking at Brett, his wife and daughter.

Melissa, dressed in a red apron adorned with dancing reindeer, multitasked effortlessly between stirring pots, and setting out plates. The kitchen island and tables are filled full of platters overflowing with delectable dishes, ready to be enjoyed by the guests.

The first arrivals, Brett and his wife, Sophie, stood near the festive table laden with finger foods. Their faces lit up with warmth and excitement, amplified by the beaming smile of their nine-year-old daughter, Lily. The trio exuded a sense of joy, their eyes twinkling with Christmas cheer.

Mark exchanged greetings with Brett and Sophie as Melissa bustled around, ensuring everything was in order. He marvelled at his wife's ability to effortlessly coordinate such an extravaganza, a testament to her love for family and the spirit of Christmas.

As the room filled with laughter and conversation, Mark could not help but notice a change in Melissa's demeanour. She would occasionally glance towards a corner of the room, her gaze lingering as if fixated on the ghost of

Mr. Fredricks. Feeling the need to investigate, Mark discreetly approached Melissa during a lull in the festivities. Leaning in closer to inquire, he whispered, "What's been capturing your attention, my love? Is Mr. Fredricks still here?"

Melissa's eyes met his, filled with a mixture of excitement and trepidation. "The ghost of Mr Fredricks finally realised that Brett is his son, and Lily, Brett's daughter, can see him to. He has been trying to communicate with them since they arrived."

"I remember you from Hell house. You were funny," Lily claimed telling the ghost of Mr. Fredricks.

"Oh, I forgot to mention that last night or early this morning since we were in a Christmas shopping rush," Mark revealed.

Mark's eyes widened, and he stared at Brett and Lily conversing animatedly with their mother Sophie. They seemed unaware of the profound link they unknowingly share. The revelation sent chills down his spine as the weight of the situation settled over him.

At eight o'clock Tom, Sarah and Patrick arrived right on time. "Greeting Garrison's," Tom announced removing his jacket and top hat. Tom whispered to Mark, "despite recent events. I did not keep my promise to help you. Therefore, to the current court restraints in place I would like to turn a new snowflake instead of melting under pressure."

Mark expressed sincerely.

"I know the Christmas lights competition means a lot to you. However, if you look online the judging panel have not taken the title away from Ravenscroft Lane and you have won first place again for the best decorated house in Gwenvale."

Tom smiled. "You mean to say, we won?"

"Congratulations Tom for your efforts working together as a community. Ravenscroft Lane is amazing, and Lily enjoyed Hell house for the money raised for dads' medical fees," Brett congratulated sounding partially reserved in his voice.

"Oh, hello Brett," Tom greeted surprised stuttering nervously for any words taken by surprise to his brother's kind words. "Hey," Brett responded.

"Time for dinner," Melissa announced cheerfully.

Ten people sat down at the lengthy table. Tom and Melissa sat at opposite ends of the table while Brett's family and Shirley sat at one side while Candy sat next to Patrick and his family at the other side. The room was quiet while Mark and Melissa began bringing out the entrées and multiple side dishes.

"I say Garrison family. This exceeds our expectations," Tom complemented staring across the table at Brett.

"I can smell a delectable, fattened turkey in the oven that Saint Niklaus couldn't finish," Brett implied. Tom laughed, "I forgot about that name."

Sophie added, "it has a romantic charm to the name that sounds manly and sophisticated."

Sarah smiled hitting Tom from under the table. "That name reminds me of father when he used to, I mean when he, um," Tom stuttered for words.

"Left, walked out and for good reason since Christmas was the reason for divorce."

Seeing the conflicts Mark and Melissa hurried the main course. "Brace yourselves for loads more food and desserts to come. Patrick and Lily conversed talking about their favourite foods. As the night continued no one was interested in eating dessert since the main course was plenty for all to eat.

"Let us all play a game in teams of two. Adults' verses everyone under the age of twenty-one and Tom can be on our team," Candy started.

"For our first game Mini winter Olympics?"

For the games ahead everyone used a basic honesty system for points, yet it seemed both brothers were more competitive than everyone else being passive participants. Patrick scored a perfect score at the snowball toss that needed a bucket and twenty cotton buds.

Sophie and Shirley tied and went to a triple sudden death in an egg and spoon race across the Livingroom. After the mini games Toms team was ahead and needing a game for everyone to play for final points. "Is anyone paying attention to me here?" The ghost of Mr Fredricks is more agitated than ever.

"Soon," Melissa reassured him as Lily surprised everyone with a game.

"Melissa and Grandpa Fredricks can judge the next game while we all play Cards against humanity Christmas Edition."

The room was dead silent for a moment. "Is it because a child is offering to play that game of all games or the fact that she said Grandpa," Sarah asked.

"Okay, don't freak out but your father has died recently, and his ghost has not crossed into the light," Mark said.

Brett and Tom both reacted not realising what has happened. "I did not know he died. Last I heard he was in hospital though I avoided him at the nursing home," Brett explained. "I, I was just too proud to visit him I never answered any private numbers since most calls are scammers. I did not he died alone, I made some poor choices to," Tom whimpered.

In a moment Candy changed the time on the grandfather clock in the living room. "Look everyone, it's past eleven seventy-five," Candy said.

Mark cringed for a moment realising his daughter still did not understand some basic life skills. "I didn't realise it was so late we are supposed to go to work at midnight."

Brett and Mark became anxious. The ghost of Mr Fredricks told Melissa to tell them both to forget about his death and focus on how you can both move forward and enjoy Christmas together once again.

"He is here, and he wants you to not dwell on his death but to find peace together and enjoy Christmas like you used to," Melissa relayed.

"How do we know you're not just making this up?" Tom was not believing Melissa. "This is a sick game and it's time for us to head home and salvage what is left of Christmas."

Melissa began relaying everything that the ghost of Mr Fredricks was saying. "Niklaus. We will tell you the story of Niklaus."

Tom and Brett listened as everyone gathered around to listen to the story of a Christmas nearly forgotten.

"Two sons, Tom, and Brett were thrilled at the prospect of gliding gracefully across the ice. However, things are not as smooth for Mom and Dad. Despite their best efforts and dozens of attempts to find their footing, they stumbled and tumbled, creating quite a comical scene. Laughter filled the rink as Dad's flailing arms resembled an uncoordinated penguin, while Mom could not help but cling to the railing for dear life. Just as frustration began to creep in, an elderly man approached. Teaching some expert tips and tricks, helping Dad steady his balance and guiding Mom in finding her rhythm. Slowly but surely, Mom and Dad began to glide with more grace and confidence, mirroring their children's earlier gracefulness. The unexpected twist he introduced himself as Santa himself incognito as Niklaus."

Brett began weeping. "He gave me my first peppermint candy cane. It was awful but it was the random act of kindness. That is why I love my job at the nursing home."

As the clock was five minutes to midnight, marking the arrival of Christmas Day, tensions brewed between Brett and his brother, Tom, adding an unexpected layer of conflict to the joyous festivities. Mark and Melissa had extended their invitation to Tom, Sarah, and their young son, Patrick, hoping to strengthen familial bonds. Little did they know, this gathering would become a battleground of emotions.

"Come on guys you need to talk this out. Your father is Earth bound and the only way to cross over is if you both can forgive each other. Can you forgive the Christmas sins so that your Christmas sins will be forgiven?" Mark said pretending to be a preacher.

"Dad did not support mom for any Christmas let alone missing each family traditions," Tom stated.

"Tell them I thought working overtime was the only way I thought I could support a family," the Ghost of Mr. Fredricks said sadly while Melissa rephrased.

Tom and Brett stood on opposite ends of the living room; their gazes locked in a silent confrontation. An air of resentment hung heavily between them, an unspoken rivalry that had festered over the years. The presence of Mr. Fredericks' ghost only served to deepen the tension as both families grappled with the profound implications of his existence.

"Come on you two. He is trying to pour his heart out if you could only hear him Say something about his working overtime," Melissa demanded while her hands gestured.

Brett opened nervously, "Lily's mother was pregnant with Lily since I made certain unprotective choices. Regardless, I waited in the room while her and her brat kid at age five went to unload things and set up Christmas. That morning when I saw the overload of presents for her kid, I quickly checked my bank account. Twenty thousand dollars spend over several days trying to make a perfect Christmas for her entitled prick of a son."

Melissa interrupted, "quickly Brett please get to your point. Your father is listening, and I think the chance to cross over is dim."

While Brett and his daughter, Lily, embraced the supernatural connection to Mr. Fredricks, Tom looked upon it with suspicion and doubt. His scepticism clashed head-on with the unwavering belief that Brett and Lily shared, creating a palpable rift between the brothers.

"I hated the selfishness and to have a daughter raised to see this selfish world of entitlement. However, to argue against myself for the sake of my marriage to Sophie and to my daughter Lily. I realised last night watching Christmas movies at work I want to teach Lily to enjoy the Christmas season not put all the pressure into one day like her mother did repetitively for her kid that shall not be named."

Lily became frantic, "its only one more minute to midnight daddy."

Sarah, Tom's wife, tried to diffuse the escalating tension in her husbands' clenched hands by holding his wrists lovingly. She knew that this night was meant to bring the family closer, but the chasm between the brothers only seemed to widen with each passing moment. Her eyes darted between her husband and her son, Patrick, who had seemingly adapted to the presence of Mr. Fredericks' ghost more easily than anyone could have expected.

"I am the asshole who did not want to celebrate Christmas and this year I wanted to let go of all that hate between us and hate that still is in my heart. I forgive you dad for not being there because I chose not to be there as well. Finally, forgive myself for allowing the past to overtake living in the present preventing Tom and I from being merry and happy," Brett sobbed.

Tom scoffed; his voice laced with bitterness. "This is not about belief, Brett. It is about-facing reality. You are clinging to some fantasy while neglecting what truly matters – our family, our present."

As the clock began to strike midnight, marking the arrival of Christmas Day, Tom clenched his eyes, fists and let out a ripper of a fart. Tom quickly responded shouting as he released tears from his eyes and another ripper of a fart. "I am also to blame for Christmases past against you Brett. I should have been there for you all and I am sorry for missing your wedding to Sophia who clearly makes you happy all year around."

"Forgive Grandpa now," yelled Lily crying as she stared at the Ghost of Mr. Fredricks crying uncontrollably holding Tom as he begged for forgiveness.

"I love you dad. You did what you could with what you knew to support us. We had a good childhood with loving parents. We all choose forgiveness."

Suddenly the ghost of Mr Fredricks gasped as a radiant light appeared that only he can see. A pulse of radiance shone through making Mr Fredricks visible to everyone while making him feel happier than any feeling he had ever know.

"I can see you Mr Fredricks," Mark gasped.

"I have never seen ghost look like a radiant shinny saint before. Or so that is what I think is happening," Gasped Melissa as everyone cried looking at Mr Fredricks.

"I see a bright light," the Ghost of Mr. Fredricks gasped. Melissa cried, "he sees the light. This means it is time for a final goodbye and he gets to Rejoyce with loved ones in Heaven on Christmas morning."

"I see paradise as far as the eye can see. Buildings made of pure gold. Loving friends from long ago are all angelic welcoming me to join them," the Ghost of Mr. Fredricks wiped his tears and went ahead toward the light. Then as fast as it came, he was sucked away unexpectedly away from the light and out of sight.

"Grandpa is gone, "Lilly screamed.

"He didn't go into the light it was like something pulled him away," Melissa cried. "I have never seen a ghost not go into the light when the light has been seen."

The words hung heavily in the air, reflecting the deep-rooted rift that had plagued the brothers for years. Their conflicting perspectives on life and the supernatural seemed to amplify their underlying grievances. The tension became an insurmountable barrier, threatening to unravel the fabric of their relationship.

Sensing the growing turbulence, Melissa and Mark glanced at each other with concern. They knew that the joy of Christmas could easily be eclipsed by the dark cloud of family strife. Determined to restore harmony, they decided to take matters into their own hands.

Melissa approached Tom; her voice gentle yet firm. "Tom, have faith in the power of love and unity. Embrace the connection that we all have discovered tonight. Let this be a night of reconciliation, not conflict."

"Quickly, everyone we need to hold hands. Candy, Shirley, and Patrick, join us," Mark ordered. "Everyone here tonight, put all scepticism aside if only for tonight on Christmas morning where we need to sing about the one true king."

All guests did not hesitate as they were steadfast in unified beliefs and the desire for familial unity. His eyes landed on Brett, who stood watching, uncertainty and hope etched on his face. With a heavy sigh, Tom finally relented. "For the sake of family, I will try."

Candy grinned. "So, who knows a Christmas carol about Jesus?" Silence was present as no one knew since modern traditions have excluded Jesus to be sang at schools or for nativity scenes to be present this time of year. "The Baptist church know, and I can call their paster now to help us," Tom said excitedly pulling out his cell phone that began rigging from a private number. "Hello, Tom Hendeson here."

Putting the phone on loudspeaker for all to hear, "You are the next of kin to a Kimberly Fredricks?"

"Yes, yes I am," he cried sobbing. "He has woken from his coma at Gwenvale General Hospital. We need to keep him here for further observations and I thought you needed to know so you can see your father for Christmas morning during visiting hours."

Crying could be heard from all around. "Thank you for telling me the good news. Tell him that his family will come by when he is ready at any time Christmas day."

"Oh, and one more thing. Happy holidays."

Candy grabbed Tom's wrist holding the phone toward her face, "it's alright to say Merry Christmas."

*   *   *

Since the Christmas party was now over and Candy revealed the actual time Mark had one final mission to do before his night shift. "Come with me Brett and Tom while we have one last drink of egg nogg before Santa comes."

"It has gotten late I should get Lilly to bed, also I need to get to work and so do you."

Tom poured a glass and raised it. "I propose a toast to Saint Niklaus and his story reminding us of true acts of kindness and goodwill to all men on earth."

"To Saint Niklaus," Mark and Brett announced tapping classes together.

"Also, to Santa, the asshole who gets all the credit each year," Mark laughed.

"Oh, speaking of Santa I have to deliver six sacks of presents since everyone has left their doors unlocked for me to enter." At that precise moment Candy, Shirley and their mother walked in carrying a sack each. "Look at this sack it has three of the latest PlayStation consoles from Santa to Riley Maurice Wolley, Lazarus Pain Casey and Judith Ravenscroft.

"Wait, what do you mean to deliver presents to each home?" Tom grimaced.

"Mr. Fredricks had a letter for me at work stating that since his injuries at home last month I had to deliver to all houses on Ravenscroft Lane this year otherwise Christmas would be cancelled. My family know your Brett I we spent far too much this Christmas and yet look at my family who enable my Christmas obsession."

Tom interrupted, "Mark, I keep it under wraps. I am the secret Santa for Ravenscroft Lane. I have been for two decades. I am going to deliver at midnight tonight."

Mark shook his head and revealed the note.

"His note was quite clear," Mark reassured.

Brett had a sudden realisation. "Wait a minute. I heard Shirley speaking about this ending for her book when I hid in the kitchen of the nursing home when dad came through. He must have gotten this idea when Shirley explained the ending to some of the residents."

"What idea Tom asked," sweating repulsively.

Brett, Tom, Mark and Mellisa rushed outside witnessing. Many men dressed as Santa delivering presents to all houses on Ravenscroft Lane. Little did anyone know Mr. Fredricks is the asshole who didn't want to celebrate Christmas. Now Mr Fredricks is remembered as the asshole who got the last laugh this Christmas and every Christmas yet to come on Ravenscroft Lane.

www.ingramcontent.com/pod-product-compliance
Lightning Source LLC
Chambersburg PA
CBHW041513120626
46551CB00018B/2406